1-5-76

Fish & Seafood Dishes

This is the sixth volume in a series designed to make the menu planner's task easier. It will open up a new world of menu variety that comes with a better understanding of fish and seafoods.

In addition to 254 recipes, the book offers suggestions for the selection, handling, and storage of all kinds of seafoods, and it outlines various methods of cooking. It also offers dozens of helpful hints, such as how to dress up any seafood dish with attractive garnishes.

Some 44 pictures illustrate the presentation of ideas for a variety of fish and seafood menu items. There are step-by-step instructions on how to prepare each dish. A helpful index adds to the usefulness of the book for the foodservice operator, supervisor, and dietitian.

Recent Titles in
Foodservice Menu Planning Series

Volume Feeding Menu Selector by Alta B. Atkinson
Eulalia C. Blair, Editor

Luncheon and Supper Dishes
Eulalia C. Blair

Salads and Salad Dressings
Eulalia C. Blair

Breakfast and Brunch Dishes
Eulalia C. Blair

Dishes for Special Occasions
Eulalia C. Blair

Fish & Seafood Dishes

FOR FOODSERVICE MENU PLANNING

Selected by

EULALIA C. BLAIR

Jule Wilkinson, Editor

CAHNERS BOOKS

A Division of Cahners Publishing Company, Inc.
89 Franklin St., Boston, Massachusetts 02110
Publishers of Institutions/VF Magazine

Library of Congress Cataloging in Publication Data
Main entry under title:

Fish & seafood dishes for foodservice menu planning.

(Foodservice menu planning series)
1. Cookery (Fish) 2. Cookery (Seafood)
3. Cookery for institutions, etc. I. Blair, Eulalia C.
TX747.F495 641.6'9 75-25636
ISBN 0-8436-2086-2

ISBN 0-8436-2086-2

Cover Picture, North Pacific Halibut Commission

Printed in the United States of America

Contents

Acknowledgements

THE RECIPES AND photographs in this book represent the generosity of many people. I wish that it were possible to list all of their names and thank them personally.

I deeply appreciate the help that has come from food processors, manufacturers, public relations firms, advertising agencies, associations, and institutions. My most sincere thanks goes out to them and to the many skilled technicians who have worked with them in developing the recipes and preparing the photographs.

I should also like to say "Thank You" to the many foodservice operators who have so graciously shared recipes from their kitchens throughout the years.

I am deeply grateful, too, for the factual information furnished by The National Fisheries Institute, and by Miss Alberta Macfarlane who so ably researched the subject of fish and shellfish in preparation of materials for Institutions Magazine.

And, once again, I want to express my appreciation to Book Editor, Jule Wilkinson for her inestimable help in handling the countless details involved in publishing this book.

EULALIA C. BLAIR

Introduction

THIS BOOK, another member of the series for foodservice planners, has to do with the exciting menu variety that can come by way of a better understanding of fish and seafood.

Toward this end, the book offers—in addition to recipes—suggestions for the selection, handling and storage of fish and seafood. It outlines the various methods of cooking and, among other tips, offers ideas for garnishes and for presenting fish portions in fancy dress.

The recipes range from the simple, homey type to the classic and gourmet. The selection, totaling more than 230, includes appetizers, soups, salads, sandwiches, and sauces as well as an extensive variety of entree items.

Chosen on the basis of their diversity, practical qualities, and potential appeal, these recipes come from the large collection of recipes which, during previous years, have appeared in the pages of Volume Feeding Management Magazine, Institutions Magazine and the combined publication, Institutions/ Volume Feeding Magazine.

Popular Fish Stories
(From top to bottom, Oven Fried Fish Fillets, Halibut Steak with Orange-Grape Sauce, Baked Trout, Island Fish Bake)

National Fisheries Institute

Fish

FISH OFFERS a fascinating variety of options for preparation and presentation that would be hard to match. This is so, first, because of the many different species and their various market forms. In addition to fish that is available fresh or frozen, there is considerable variety among canned fish items. Tuna, salmon, and sardines are, of course, regular standbys. Other canned items, possibly less familiar, include spiced and pickled herring, anchovies, fish flakes, and kippers. We find a surprisingly extensive selection in our present-day markets.

In addition, there are the different methods of cooking fish that can bring about many a pleasing change. There is also a diversity of dishes that can be prepared with fish, an assortment which takes in sandwiches, soups, and salads as well as appetizers and entree features.

Besides, there are innumerable possibilities with seasonings, sauces, accompaniments, and garnishes that can individualize the presentation of fish dishes, extend their variety, and make them a focal point on the menu.

Market Forms of Fin Fish

MOST MARKET FORMS of fish are familiar to foodservice operators. However, as a brief review lest any piscatorial menu potential be overlooked:

WHOLE OR ROUND FISH (Fresh)	Whole, uncut fish just as they come from the water.
DRAWN FISH (Fresh or Frozen)	Whole fish that have been eviscerated. Scales, head, fins, and tail are intact.
DRESSED OR PAN-DRESSED (Fresh or Frozen)	Scaled, trimmed, and ready to cook.
STEAKS (Fresh or Frozen)	Cross-section cuts of large fish, usually cut 3/4 to 1 in. thick.
FILLETS (Fresh or Frozen)	Sides of fish cut away from the bones. (*Flitches* are fillets from a large fish cut 14 in. in length.)
BUTTERFLY FILLETS (Fresh or Frozen)	Fillets cut from the two sides of a fish, kept as a single piece held together by uncut flesh and skin.
BREADED FILLETS (Frozen, Raw or Cooked)	Fillets coated with a seasoned breading.
BREADED PORTIONS (Frozen, Raw or Cooked)	Uniform serving portions (squares, rectangles, or fillet shapes) cut from blocks of frozen fillets. Coated with a seasoned breading.
FISH STICKS (Frozen, Raw or Cooked)	Uniform sticks cut from blocks of frozen fillets. Coated with a seasoned breading.

Handling and Storage

FISH IS ONE of the most delicate and perishable of foods. Ideally, fish to be marketed fresh is packed in ice as soon as caught, then shipped under refrigeration to arrive at its destination in the shortest possible time after leaving the water.

Once purchased, the fish must be kept refrigerated until preparation time. It should not be held for more than one or two days.

Frozen fish should be stored in the freezer at zero degrees or lower until ready to thaw or cook. At these temperatures it can be kept for several months.

All frozen products that come prepared with breading should be cooked while solidly frozen. They should go directly from freezer to fryer or oven.

Unbreaded products may also be cooked without thawing. But if they are to be rolled or stuffed or coated with a breading before cooking, it will facilitate handling to thaw the fish until the portions separate easily.

*To thaw, place individual packages in a refrigerator at 35°
to 40°F. Allow 24 to 36 hours for 1-lb. packages, 48 to 72
hours for 5-lb. packages. For quicker thawing, place individual packages in water-tight wrapping under cold running
water. Allow one to two hours for 1-lb. packages, and two
to three hours for 5-lb. packages.* Do not thaw *at room temperature or in warm water.*

After thawing, do not refreeze. Hold the fish in a refrigerator and use within 24 hours.

From Freezer to Fryer for Maximum Appeal

Bureau of Commercial Fisheries, USDA

Fish Cookery

FISH COOKS more quickly than almost any other food. But remember that fish is, by nature, a delicate, tender product. It needs to be treated gently. To insure serving at the peak of perfection—tender, tasty, and moist—hold strictly to the one cardinal rule: Do not overcook. *Then one more word of caution: Frozen pre-cooked items are already cooked and need only to be reheated. Do not make the mistake of cooking them twice and, in consequence, downgrading taste and texture.*

Fish is without tough fibers that take considerable cooking time to become tender and soft. The protein of fish is, actually, quite similar to that of an egg. It needs only a small amount of heat to firm it up. When cooked beyond that point, the flesh behaves like an egg; it gets overly firm, starts to dry out and toughen.

Fish is done when it "flakes" or, in other words, when, probed with a fork at the thickest part, the flesh slides easily at its natural divisions or "markings." For another doneness cue, observe when the flesh becomes opaque and no longer has a shiny look. To be moist, hot, and fully flavorful, fish must be served as soon as it is ready.

Fish lends itself to baking, broiling, frying, sauteing, poaching, and steaming. Each cooking method produces a different effect and allows ample margin for drama and change.

Most market forms are suitable for broiling. Steaks and fillets take kindly to sauteing or baking. Small whole fish are well-suited for the saute method. Some small whole fish are especially attractive when stuffed and baked. Portions that come breaded, ready to cook, fare best when deep fat fried or prepared in the oven. Pre-cooked breaded portions are best suited for oven finishing.

Poaching is a favorite method for large whole fish. This method also works well for fillets. The thinner ones, pliable enough to fold or roll for poaching, can provide the starting point for many an unusual and elegant dish.

Steaming or poaching is recommended for cooking thick fillets to be used as flaked fish (for making fish pies, souffles, salads, casseroles, creamed, or a la King dishes, etc.).

TO BAKE, *simply arrange the pieces of fish in an oiled pan, brush with butter or margarine and cook (at 350° to 400°F. in a regular oven or at 300° to 325°F. in a convection oven), basting occasionally with plain or seasoned butter until just cooked through.*

Curry, bay leaf, onion, parsley, marjoram, and thyme are among the many seasonings that enhance baked fish. A little paprika encourages browning when sprinkled over the top of a pale-fleshed fish before baking. The added color enhances the appearance of the finished dish.

Other ways to achieve flavor variation include baking fish in dry white wine, light cream, or a sauce.

Fish prepared with stuffing is a popular variant of oven-cooked fish. A stuffing can fill the cavity of a whole fish; be used between two fillets, or line the inside of a rolled fillet.

Baking holds a definite advantage when it is necessary to have a large number of portions ready to serve at one time.

BROILING *is another of the easy ways to cook fish. It is no problem at all to prepare portions (placed skin side down) on a piece of heavy foil, a well-oiled rack or pan, or a broil-*

and-serve platter. Brush the fish generously with butter, margarine, or oil, putting on a bit extra if the fish is lean. While cooking, baste with melted butter or a mixture of butter and lemon juice or white wine.

Adding a well-chosen herb to the butter for basting is a clever way of introducing seasoning. Marinating the fish prior to broiling, then using the marinade for basting, provides another means of varying the flavor scheme.

FRYING *in deep fat is a popular method of cooking fish. For best results, use a fryer with a fast temperature recovery and a fresh, bland shortening or oil. Fry in fat heated to 350° to 375°F. until just done. Avoid overloading the fryer by attempting to cook too much fish at one time.*

Fish for deep frying must be dipped in milk or other liquid and coated with a breading, or dipped in a thin batter. When cooking frozen ready-breaded fish, it is important to put it in the fryer in the frozen state. Do not thaw.

SAUTEING *or panfrying also requires dipping the fish in milk, then in seasoned flour corn meal, or other breading material. Cook in a heavy skillet containing a layer of hot oil about 1/8 in. deep. Saute over moderate heat, turning once to brown both sides.*

POACHING *fish means gentle simmering in water, court bouillon, or other seasoned liquid. The technique specifies a shallow pan and an amount of liquid to barely cover the fish. Bring the liquid to a simmer, cover the fish with a piece of waxed paper or buttered brown paper, cut to fit the pan. Cook on top of the range or in the oven, keeping the liquid to a simmer (below the boiling point) until the fish is done.*

The liquid from the poaching is often reduced and then thickened to make a sauce to dress the poached fish and complete the dish.

STEAMING *calls for cooking in a steam cooker or in a covered utensil, with the fish resting on a rack placed above the level of the boiling water. To calculate the cooking time for steaming, measure the fish at its thickest part and allow 10 minutes for each measured inch.*

OVEN FINISHING *is the recommended procedure for heating frozen, pre-cooked, breaded items. Place on shallow ungreased baking sheet; follow package directions for time and temperature.*

Shellfish

Species	Other Names	Where Caught	Market Forms
Clams			
Butter		Pacific Coast, Alaska	
Hard	Hard Shell, Cherry-stones, Quahog	New England, Middle and South Atlantic	
Little Neck		Pacific Coast, Alaska	
Razor		Pacific Coast, Alaska	Live in shell
Soft	Soft Shell	New England, Middle Atlantic, Pacific	Shucked, fresh and frozen
Surf	Skimmer	Middle Atlantic	Frozen breaded, raw and cooked
*Geoduck	King Clam, Gweduc, Gwee duk, Gooey-duck	Washington's Puget Sound, South of Anacortes and in Hood Canal	Canned
*Ocean Quahog	Mahogany quahog, Mahogany clam, Black quahog	New England Coast	
Crabs			
Blue		Middle and South Atlantic, Gulf	
Dungeness		Pacific Coast, Alaska	Live in shell
King		Alaska	Fresh or frozen:
Stone		Florida, Texas	Cooked meat, sections,
Snow	Tanner, Queen	Pacific Coast, Alaska	claws
*Jonah		New England Coast from Maine to	Specialties:

		Cape Hatteras, North Carolina	Frozen breaded, raw, cooked (cakes, patties, deviled, stuffed, etc.)
*Red	Deep Sea Red Crab	New England and Middle Atlantic Coast	Canned
Lobsters			
Northern	Maine	New England, Canada	Live in shell
Rock		South Africa, Australia	Fresh or frozen: Cooked meat, cooked whole, tails raw
Spiny		Europe, Australia, North America South America, Japan, Africa	Canned
Mussels	Bay Mussels	New England and Middle Atlantic	Live in shell, frozen in sauces, canned
Oysters			
Eastern		New England, Middle and South Atlantic, Gulf	Live in shell; shucked, fresh, frozen; frozen breaded raw or fried, canned, smoked
Pacific	Japanese	Pacific Coast, Japan, Korea	
Olympia	Western	Pacific Coast	
Scallops			
Bay		Middle and South Atlantic, Gulf	Fresh or frozen: Shucked
Calico		South Atlantic	Frozen breaded, raw or cooked
Sea		New England	Specialties

*Available on a regional basis

(Cont.)

Shellfish

Species	Other Names	Where Caught	Market Forms
Shrimp			
White	Prawn	South Atlantic, Gulf	Fresh or frozen: Raw, headless Peeled (including deveined), raw or cooked Frozen breaded, raw or fried Cooked whole Canned
Brown and Pink		South Atlantic, Gulf	
Alaska Pink		Alaska	
Bay		Maine, Mexico, French Guinea, Dutch Guinea (imports virtually world-wide)	
*Rock		Gulf of Mexico off Yucatan Peninsula near Contoy. Limited extent Cape Kennedy area on Florida East Coast and on Northwest Coast near Apalachicola, Florida	Packaged; split-in-the-shell
Squid	Inkfish, Bone Squid, Calamari, Calamary, Sea Arrow, Flying Squid, Taw Taw	Atlantic, Gulf and Southern California	Frozen; canned

*Available on a regional basis

Source: National Fisheries Institute

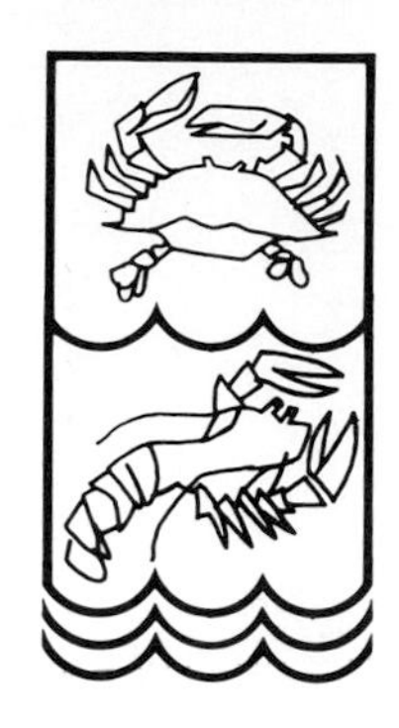

Seafood

IN THIS AGE of the jet and modern processing methods, the bounty of the sea can be enjoyed in some form no matter where. The fabulous shellfish family—clams, crab, lobster, mussels, oysters, scallops, shrimp, and snails—can make a contribution to your menu at any season, almost any time of day.

Each type of seafood has a character of its own. Still, many recipes permit interchanging two or even three varieties. And others allow leeway for combinations.

Shellfish, like fin fish, cook quickly and begin to toughen once cooking proceeds beyond the just-done stage. The same firm rule applies: Cook for the shortest possible time and serve at once. Seafood that comes already cooked should be gently heated, not subjected to cooking a second time.

Suggestions for Fish and Seafood Appetizers

CLAMS

Cold:

- On the half shell
- Raw clam cocktail
- Minced clam dip

Hot:

- Steamed clams

CRAB

Cold:

- Crab stuffed eggs
- Crab canapes
- Crabmeat cocktail
- Crabmeat and artichoke cocktail
- Crabmeat and avocado cocktail
- Crab stuffed avocado
- Curried crabmeat dip

Hot:

- Creamed crab in miniature pastry shells
- Crabmeat turnovers
- Mushroom caps stuffed with crabmeat
- Crepes filled with sherried crabmeat
- Petite crabmeat croquettes

FISH

Cold:

- Anchovy stuffed eggs
- Egg and anchovy canape
- Tomato and anchovy canape
- Flaked fish cocktail
- Flaked fish in aspic
- Marinated fish (Seviche)
- Pickled herring
- Marinated herring and sweet onion rings
- Herring in sour cream
- Sardine and egg canape
- Sardine and cucumber canape
- Sardine and tomato canape
- Gefilte fish with horseradish
- Halibut cubes (cut from cold poached fish) in cocktail sauce
- Smoked salmon
- Salmon stuffed eggs
- Tuna cocktail
- Tuna and orange cocktail
- Tuna chunks in lettuce cup, served with lemon wedges

Hot:

- Codfish balls with hot chili sauce
- Broiled sardine canape

LOBSTER

Cold:

- Lobster with orange sections
- Chilled cracked lobster claws
- Lobster and avocado appetizer

Hot:
- Lobster-filled crepes

MUSSELS

Cold:
- Pickled mussels
- Smoked mussels
- Stuffed mussels

OYSTERS

Cold:
- On the half shell
  (For something special, add a dab of red or black caviar, placed on top of each oyster)
- Oyster cocktail

Hot:
- Oysters Rockefeller

SCALLOPS

Cold:
- Diced poached scallops in a spicy cocktail sauce
- Marinated cooked scallops
- Raw scallops marinated in lemon or lime juice (Scallops Seviche)

SEAFOOD COMBINATIONS

Cold:
- Seafood cocktail
- Citrus and seafood cocktail
- Seafood and diced avocado cocktail

SHRIMP

Cold:
- Shrimp and celery cocktail
- Shrimp as a cocktail with:
  - Grapefruit
  - Pineapple
  - Avocado
  - Oranges
  - Cucumber
  - Tomato

- Small tomatoes stuffed with marinated shrimp
- Iced shrimp in a dill marinade
- Pickled shrimp
- Shrimp served with a dip
- Shrimp in aspic on cress
- Shrimp and cheese dip
- Shrimp and tomato wedges in a parsley and dill sauce

Hot:
- Sauteed tiny shrimp in toast cup
- Broiled skewered shrimp
- Fried shrimp with hot mustard sauce
- Tempura shrimp
- Shrimp in a creamy dill sauce served in a small pastry tart shell

Peach and Shrimp Remoulade

Cling Peach Advisory Board

NORTH PACIFIC HALIBUT KABOBS

Yield: 24 kabobs

Ingredients

HALIBUT, FLITCH or STEAK, cut bite size	2 pounds
GREEN PEPPERS, cut into square pieces	4
CHERRY TOMATOES	24
MUSHROOM CAPS, MEDIUM SIZE	24
BASTING SAUCE*	as needed

Procedure

1. Thread halibut, peppers, tomatoes, and mushroom caps on skewers.
2. Brush with basting sauce. Broil, basting frequently and turning to brown evenly on all sides.

*BASTING SAUCE

Yield: 1 cup

Ingredients

SALAD OIL	1/4 cup
SOY SAUCE	1/4 cup
LEMON JUICE	1 tablespoon
SUGAR	1 tablespoon
TOMATO JUICE	1/2 cup
DRY MUSTARD	1/2 teaspoon
SALT	as needed

Procedure

1. Combine oil, soy sauce, lemon juice, sugar, and tomato juice.
2. Add dry mustard and salt to taste.
3. Mix until well blended.

Pineapple Salad Pie (see recipe, facing page)

Dole Company

JELLIED TUNA COCKTAIL

Yield: 40 1/2-cup portions

Ingredients

GELATIN, LEMON FLAVOR	1-1/2 pounds (3-1/2 cups)
SALT	2 tablespoons
CAYENNE PEPPER	1/4 teaspoon
TOMATO JUICE, hot	3 quarts (1 No. 10 can)
LEMON JUICE	1/4 cup
HORSERADISH	3 tablespoons
ONION, grated	3 tablespoons
TUNA, flaked	1-1/4 pounds (1 quart)
CELERY, chopped	1 quart

Procedure

1. Dissolve gelatin, salt, and cayenne in hot tomato juice. Cool. Add lemon juice. Chill until slightly thickened.
2. Fold in horseradish, grated onion, tuna, and celery
3. Pour into individual molds or shallow pans. Chill until firm.
4. Unmold or cut into squares. Serve on crisp greens. Garnish with mayonnaise blended with sour cream, if desired.

PINEAPPLE SALAD PIE

(See picture, facing page)

Yield: 6 9-inch pies

Ingredients	
PINEAPPLE, CRUSHED	1 No. 10 can
PINEAPPLE SYRUP and WATER	7-1/2 cups
GELATIN, LEMON FLAVOR	1-1/2 pounds
TOMATO SAUCE	2-1/2 cups
WHITE VINEGAR, DISTILLED	1/2 cup
SALT	1 tablespoon
PEPPER	1/4 teaspoon
HORSERADISH	2 to 3 tablespoons
INSTANT CHOPPED ONION	2 tablespoons
PINEAPPLE, CRUSHED, drained	2 quarts
PASTRY SHELLS, 9-inch, baked	6
SHRIMP, cooked, cleaned	as needed
TARTAR SAUCE, PREPARED	1 quart
PINEAPPLE, CRUSHED, drained	1 cup

Procedure

1. Drain pineapple. Measure syrup; add water to make required amount of liquid.
2. Heat liquid to boiling; pour over gelatin; stir to dissolve.
3. Blend in tomato sauce, vinegar, salt, pepper, horseradish, and onion. Chill until slightly thickened. Fold in first amount of drained pineapple.
4. Turn mixture into pie shells, allowing 3 cups per shell. Garnish with shrimp, arranging around edge of shell. Chill until firm.
5. Cut into wedges to serve as an appetizer or as salad entree.
6. Combine tartar sauce and remaining crushed pineapple. Serve as a dressing with the wedges of pie.

SHRIMP CANAPE →

Yield: 36 canapes

Ingredients

SHRIMP, CANNED or cooked, shelled, deveined, chopped	1-1/2 pounds (ready-to-use weight)
ANCHOVY PASTE	2 tablespoons
LEMON JUICE	2 tablespoons
MAYONNAISE	1 cup
TOAST ROUNDS, 2-inch	36
EGGS, hard-cooked, yolks sieved	8
SHRIMP, WHOLE, cooked, shelled, deveined	36

CREOLE SHRIMP REMOULADE

Yield: 24 portions

Ingredients

CELERY, finely cut	1-1/2 cups
ONION, chopped	1-1/2 cups
PARSLEY, chopped	1-1/2 cups
DILL PICKLE, chopped	1-1/2 cups
GARLIC, minced	2 tablespoons
PREPARED HOT MUSTARD	3-1/2 cups
HORSERADISH	1/3 cup
VINEGAR	1/2 cup
SALAD OIL	1/2 cup
SHRIMP, cooked	6 pounds
LETTUCE, shredded	3 quarts

Procedure

1. Combine celery, onion, parsley, dill pickle, garlic, prepared mustard, horseradish, vinegar, and salad oil. Mix well. Chill.
2. For each portion, arrange 4 ounces of shrimp on 1/2 cup shredded lettuce; top with 1/3 cup sauce.

Procedure

1. Combine chopped shrimp, anchovy paste, lemon juice, and mayonnaise; toss to mix.
2. Spread on toast rounds. Top with sieved egg yolk and whole shrimp.
3. Serve garnished with a celery heart and a tomato wedge arranged on a small lettuce leaf.

RIPE OLIVE SHRIMP QUICHE

Yield: 5 9-inch quiche

Ingredients

ONION, finely chopped	6 ounces
BUTTER or MARGARINE	4 ounces
SHRIMP, RAW, shelled, deveined	1 pound, 10 ounces
HALF-AND-HALF or LIGHT CREAM	2-1/2 quarts
SALT	1-1/2 tablespoons
DILL WEED	1-1/4 teaspoons
PEPPER	1/2 teaspoon
OLIVES, RIPE, SLICED, drained	10 ounces (2-1/2 cups)
EGGS, beaten	2-1/2 pounds
QUICHE PANS, 9-inch, lined with pie pastry	5
CHEESE, SWISS, grated	10 ounces

Procedure

1. Saute onion in butter until soft but not browned.
2. Chop shrimp coarsely. Add to onion mixture; cook until pink.
3. Add half-and-half, seasonings, and ripe olives; heat to simmering. Blend into beaten eggs.
4. Bake pastry-lined quiche shells in oven at 400°F. for 10 minutes. Fill partially baked shells with custard mixture, allowing approximately 1 quart per quiche. Sprinkle each with 2 ounces of cheese.
5. Continue baking 25 minutes or longer, or until filling is set.
6. Allow baked quiche to set 10 minutes before cutting.

SHRIMP ALICANTE

Yield: 12 portions

Ingredients

SHRIMP, LARGE, RAW	2-1/2 pounds
ORANGES, LARGE, peeled	6
ONIONS, peeled	1-1/2 pounds
SUGAR	1/4 cup
SALT	1-1/2 tablespoons
PEPPER	1/2 teaspoon
MUSTARD SEED	2 teaspoons
CELERY SEED	1 teaspoon
RED PEPPER, CRUSHED	1/2 teaspoon
SWEET PEPPER FLAKES	2 tablespoons
PARSLEY, FRESH, chopped	2 tablespoons
GARLIC, crushed	2 cloves
CIDER VINEGAR	1-1/2 cups
SALAD OIL	1 cup
LEMON JUICE, fresh	2/3 cup
CATSUP	1/2 cup

Procedure

1. Cook, shell, and devein shrimp.
2. Cut each orange into 3 or 4 thick slices; cut each slice into quarters.
3. Slice onions; separate into rings.
4. Combine shrimp, oranges, and onions in a large bowl.
5. Combine remaining ingredients; mix thoroughly. Pour over shrimp mixture. Cover; marinate 2 days in refrigerator, stirring twice each day.
6. Drain before serving as an hors d'oeuvre or on lettuce as an appetizer course.

Soups

Soup with Savor of the Sea
(Upper left, Mock She-Crab Soup, a favorite in the Old South; below, Creole Fish Fillets with Southern Fried Potatoes)

National Fisheries Institute/Frozen Potato Products Institute

ALASKA KING CRAB SWEET CORN CHOWDER 

Yield: 24 portions

Ingredients	
GREEN PEPPER, diced	1/2 cup
CELERY, diced	1/2 cup
ONION, chopped	1/2 cup
BUTTER or MARGARINE	2 ounces
CORN, KERNEL, CANNED	2 cups
PIMIENTO, diced	1/2 cup
FISH STOCK	2 quarts
SALT	2 to 3 teaspoons
CAYENNE PEPPER	dash
MONOSODIUM GLUTAMATE	1 tablespoon
CORNSTARCH	1/2 cup
MILK, CONCENTRATED, SKIM	2 cups
KING CRABMEAT	2 pounds

Alaska King Crab Sweet Corn Chowder (Recipe above)

Alaska King Crab Marketing and Quality Control

Procedure

1. Saute green pepper, celery, and onion in butter until transparent.
2. Add corn, pimiento, fish stock, and seasonings; simmer 10 minutes.
3. Blend cornstarch with milk; stir into stock mixture. Cook, stirring gently, until slightly thickened.
4. Carefully add crabmeat.
5. Serve in abalone shells set in rock salt.* Serve with sesame bread sticks, if desired.

*Or in warm soup bowls.

MANHATTAN CLAM CHOWDER

Yield: 3 gallons

Ingredients

ONION, chopped	4 ounces (1 cup)
SHORTENING	2 tablespoons
TOMATO JUICE	1 No. 10 can (3 quarts)
CLAM LIQUOR and WATER to equal	1-1/4 gallons
CELERY, chopped	1 pound (1 quart)
INSTANT SLICED POTATOES	1 pound, 2 ounces
SALT	2 tablespoons
PEPPER	1/2 teaspoon
CLOVES, WHOLE	8
THYME	2 to 3 teaspoons
BAY LEAVES	4
TOMATOES, CANNED	1-3/4 quarts
CLAMS, MINCED	3-1/2 pounds (3 quarts)
PARSLEY, chopped	1/3 cup

Procedure

1. Saute onion in shortening until tender but not browned. Add tomato juice, liquid, celery, potatoes, and seasonings. Cover; simmer 15 minutes.
2. Add tomatoes and clams. Simmer 15 minutes longer, or until clams are tender. Just before serving, add chopped parsley.

SHRIMP SOUP LOUISIANE

Yield: 6 gallons

Ingredients	
GREEN PEPPER, seeded	1-1/2 pounds
CELERY	1-1/2 pounds
ONION, SPANISH	1-1/2 pounds
GARLIC	1 ounce
PARSLEY	2 ounces
SHORTENING	1/2 pound
BACON FAT	6 ounces
TOMATOES	4 No. 10 cans
TOMATO PUREE	1 No. 10 can
SHRIMP STOCK	1 gallon
VINEGAR	1/4 cup
BAY LEAVES	2
PEPPERCORNS	10
SALT	4 ounces
THYME	1 ounce
WORCESTERSHIRE SAUCE	1/2 cup
SUGAR	10 ounces
LIQUID HOT PEPPER SEASONING	4 dashes
MONOSODIUM GLUTAMATE	1 ounce
SHRIMP SHELLS from 5 pounds of cleaned raw shrimp	
FLOUR	12 ounces
WATER	2 quarts
SHRIMP, SMALL, cooked	5 to 7 pounds

Procedure

1. Chop or grind green pepper, celery, onion, garlic, and parsley.
2. Melt shortening and bacon fat together. Saute vegetables until soft. **Do not brown.**
3. Combine sauteed vegetable mixture with tomatoes, tomato puree, shrimp stock (from previously cooked shrimp), vinegar, and other seasonings. Add the shrimp shells (wrapped in a cheesecloth bag); simmer slowly for 1 hour.
4. Blend the flour and water, add to the hot liquid, stirring constantly. Let simmer for 1 hour longer. Remove shells.
5. To serve, place a few small whole shrimp, or shrimp split in two lengthwise, in warm soup dish. Ladle 6 to 8 ounces of soup over shrimp.

HEARTY SALMON CHOWDER

Yield: 1-3/4 gallons

Ingredients

ONION, finely chopped	1-1/4 cups
BUTTER or MARGARINE	3 ounces
CREAM of MUSHROOM SOUP, CONDENSED	2 50-ounce cans
MILK	1 soup can
WATER	1 soup can
SALMON, drained, flaked	2 pounds
PARSLEY, chopped	2/3 cup
WHITE PEPPER	1/4 teaspoon
PAPRIKA	1/4 teaspoon

Procedure

1. Cook onion in butter until tender but not brown.
2. Blend in soup, milk, water, salmon, parsley, and pepper. Heat, but do not boil.
3. Serve garnished with paprika.

LOBSTER STEW

Yield: approximately 2-1/2 quarts

Ingredients

BUTTER or MARGARINE	1/2 pound
SALT	3/4 teaspoon
PAPRIKA	1/2 teaspoon
CELERY SALT	1-1/2 teaspoons
WORCESTERSHIRE SAUCE	1-1/2 tablespoons
CLAM BROTH or BOTTLED CLAM JUICE	3 cups
LOBSTER MEAT (or tail and claw meat from 3 medium-sized boiled lobsters)	1-1/2 pounds
MILK	1 quart
CREAM	2 cups

Procedure

1. Melt butter in a very hot kettle or pot (preferably heavy cast aluminum). Add salt, paprika, celery salt, Worcestershire sauce, and clam broth; bring to a boil.
2. Add lobster meat, milk, and cream. Bring quickly to the boiling point again, removing from heat before it actually begins to boil.
3. Serve in warmed individual soup bowls as quickly as possible, topping each portion with a pat of butter and a sprinkling of paprika.

SEASHORE CHOWDER →

Yield: 30 8-ounce portions

Ingredients

ONION, finely chopped	2 cups
BUTTER or MARGARINE	1/4 cup (2 ounces)
CREAM of CELERY SOUP, CONDENSED	1 50-ounce can
WATER	2 soup cans
CLAM CHOWDER	1 52-ounce can
FISH, cooked, boned, flaked	1 quart (2 pounds)
PARSLEY, chopped	1/4 cup

SHRIMP GUMBO

Yield: 50 8-ounce portions

Ingredients

WATER or FISH STOCK*	2 gallons
SHRIMP, RAW, shelled, deveined	2 pounds
GREEN PEPPER, chopped	2 cups
OKRA	1 No. 2 can
ONION, chopped	3 cups
TOMATOES	1 No. 10 can
SALT	1-1/2 tablespoons
PEPPER	1/2 teaspoon
BUTTER or MARGARINE	6 ounces
FLOUR	1-1/2 cups (6 ounces)
RICE, cooked	3 cups

*To make fish stock: Add shrimp shells, several celery stalks with leaves, 3 sliced carrots, and 3 sliced onions to 2 gallons of water. Simmer, covered, for 30 to 45 minutes; strain.

Procedure

1. Combine water or stock, uncooked shrimp, green pepper, okra, onion, tomatoes, sugar, salt, and pepper. Bring to a boil; simmer 10 minutes.

2. Melt butter; blend in flour. Add to soup mixture. Cook, stirring gently, until slightly thickened.

3. Add cooked rice; simmer 5 minutes.

Procedure

1. Cook onion in butter until tender but not brown.
2. Blend in soup and water; stir until smooth.
3. Add clam chowder and remaining ingredients; heat.

CLAM CHOWDER

Yield: 9 quarts

Ingredients

CLAMS, shucked, cooked in liquor, chopped	1-1/2 quarts
CLAM BROTH and WATER to equal	2 quarts
SALT PORK, finely diced	1 pound
ONION, MEDIUM, thinly sliced	1-1/2 pounds
POTATOES, finely diced	1 pound
BUTTER	1/4 pound
FLOUR	3 ounces (3/4 cup)
MILK	3 quarts
SALT	as needed
PEPPER	as needed

Procedure

1. Drain clam broth from clams cooked in their own liquor. Add water to broth to make 2 quarts.
2. Cook salt pork until crisp. Drain off all but 4 tablespoons of fat. Add onion; saute until tender and yellow.
3. Add clam broth and water, and potatoes. Cook, covered, until potatoes are tender, about 15 minutes.
4. Melt butter in heavy saucepan. Add flour; blend. Pour in milk all at once; immediately stir vigorously with whisk over moderate heat. Cook and stir until thickened.
5. Add potato and onion mixture and the chopped clams. Season. Heat gently, stirring frequently, until hot.

SHRIMP CHOWDER

Yield: 14 8-ounce portions

Ingredients

ONION, sliced	1 cup
BUTTER or MARGARINE	2 tablespoons
CREAM of CELERY SOUP, CONDENSED	1 50-ounce can
WATER	1 soup can
SHRIMP, cooked, diced	2 cups*
MARJORAM or CURRY POWDER	as needed

*1 pound shrimp before cooking.

Procedure

1. Cook onion in butter until tender.
2. Blend in soup and water.
3. Add shrimp and seasoning to taste; heat.

BY-THE-SEA CHOWDER

Yield: 3-1/2 quarts

Ingredients

CELERY, sliced 1/8 to 1/4 inch	1-1/4 cups
ONION, chopped	1 cup
BUTTER or MARGARINE	2 tablespoons
TOMATO RICE SOUP, CONDENSED	1 51-ounce can
WATER	1 soup can
LEMON JUICE	2 tablespoons
INSTANT GRANULATED GARLIC	1/8 to 1/4 teaspoon
THYME, LEAF, CRUSHED	1/8 to 1/4 teaspoon
FISH, COD, HADDOCK or HALIBUT, cooked, flaked	2 cups (8 ounces)
SHERRY, DRY (optional)	2 to 4 tablespoons
PARSLEY, chopped	as needed

Procedure

1. Saute celery and onion in butter until onion is tender.
2. Stir in soup, water, lemon juice, garlic, thyme, and fish.
3. Heat to boiling; simmer 5 minutes to blend flavor.
4. Add sherry, if desired. Garnish with parsley.

BURRIDA (GENOESE FISH STEW)

Yield: 48 portions

Ingredients	
SALT CODFISH	4 pounds
WATER, cold	as needed
INSTANT ONION FLAKES	1 quart
INSTANT MINCED GARLIC	2-1/2 tablespoons
WATER	3 cups
OLIVE or SALAD OIL	2-2/3 cups
TOMATOES, broken up	1 No. 10 can
DRY WHITE WINE	2-1/2 quarts
WALNUTS, finely chopped or ground	2 cups
PARSLEY FLAKES	1 cup
BAY LEAVES	6
RED PEPPER, GROUND	1 teaspoon
SALMON, cut into 2-inch pieces	8 pounds
MACKEREL FILLETS, cut into 2-inch pieces	8 pounds

Procedure

1. Place codfish in cold water to cover; let soak for several hours. Drain. Cut into 2-inch pieces.
2. Add onion flakes and garlic to measured (fresh) water; let stand 10 minutes to rehydrate.
3. Saute vegetables in oil for 5 minutes.
4. Remove from heat. Add tomatoes, wine, walnuts, parsley flakes, bay leaves, and red pepper. Bring to a boil and boil rapidly, uncovered, 5 minutes.
5. Add fish. Reduce heat; cover; cook 20 minutes or until fish flakes when tested with a fork.
6. Serve with slices of toasted bread, if desired.

SHRIMP GAZPACHO

Yield: 24 8-ounce portions, 2 to 4 shrimp

Ingredients

SHRIMP, MEDIUM, cooked, shelled, deveined	3 pounds
TOMATOES, FRESH, diced	24
CUCUMBERS, peeled, diced	12
GREEN PEPPERS, chopped	4
ONIONS, MEDIUM, chopped	4
WATERCRESS, chopped	1-1/4 cups
TOMATO JUICE	2 quarts
OLIVE OIL	1 cup
VINEGAR	1 cup
LIQUID HOT PEPPER SEASONING	1/4 teaspoon
GARLIC, crushed	2 cloves
SALT	as needed
CAYENNE PEPPER	as needed

Procedure

1. Combine ingredients, seasoning with salt and cayenne pepper as needed.
2. Chill thoroughly.

Note

For buffet service, place in a large bowl. Garnish top with additional shrimp.

QUICK CLAM CHOWDER

Yield: 50 3/4-cup portions

Ingredients

SALT PORK or BACON, diced	8 ounces
ONION, chopped	4 ounces
CLAMS, CANNED, MINCED	2 quarts
POTATOES, cooked, diced	3 pounds
SALT	2 tablespoons
MILK	2 gallons

Procedure

1. Saute salt pork and onion together for 5 minutes. Add to the clams.
2. Combine mixture with potatoes, salt, and milk. Heat thoroughly, but do not allow to boil.

Sandwiches

Pimiento Cheese Sandwiches with Crab Chunks

Associated Pimiento Canners

Toasted Maine Sardine-Cheese Sandwich

Maine Sardine Council; Cling Peach Advisory Board

SHRIMP SALAD ROLL

Yield: 40 portions, 1 No. 12 scoop salad mixture per portion

Ingredients

SHRIMP, cooked, coarsely chopped	3 quarts
CELERY, diced	1-1/2 quarts
ONION, finely chopped	3 tablespoons
MAYONNAISE	2 cups
LEMON JUICE	1/3 cup
SALT	1-1/2 tablespoons
PEPPER	1/4 teaspoon
FRANKFURTER ROLLS, toasted	40
ROMAINE	as needed

Procedure

1. Combine shrimp, celery, onion, mayonnaise, lemon juice, salt, and pepper. Mix thoroughly. Chill.
2. Cut rolls lengthwise, about 2/3 of way through. Spread open. Place cut surfaces up, on baking pan; toast under broiler.
3. Arrange romaine leaf on each open roll; place No. 12 scoop of shrimp salad on top. Spread evenly over both sides of roll. Serve with Dill Sauce.*

*DILL SAUCE

Yield: 5 cups

Ingredients

SOUR CREAM	1 quart
DILL PICKLE, chopped	1 cup
PARSLEY, chopped	1/4 cup

Procedure

1. Combine all ingredients. Chill.

CRABMEAT UNDER A CLOUD

Yield: 45 portions

Ingredients

ENRICHED BREAD, fresh or day-old	45 slices
CREAM of CELERY SOUP, CONDENSED	1-1/2 50-ounce cans (2-1/8 quarts)
GREEN PEPPER, chopped	1-1/2 cups
CRABMEAT, flaked	2 pounds, 7 ounces *or* 3 No. 1 flat cans
EGG YOLKS	8 ounces
SHERRY	1/2 cup
EGG WHITES	1 pound
SUGAR	6 tablespoons
LEMON JUICE	3 tablespoons

Procedure

1. Trim crusts from bread. Arrange 15 slices of bread on the bottom of each of 3 greased 12-inch by 20-inch by 2-1/2-inch steam table pans, fitting them close together.
2. Combine soup, green pepper, crabmeat, and egg yolks in a saucepan. Bring to a boil over low heat, stirring frequently. Add sherry.
3. Spoon an even amount of crabmeat mixture over bread, using about 1/3 cup for each sandwich.
4. Beat egg whites until frothy. Sprinkle sugar and lemon juice over top; continue to beat until meringue stands in peaks.
5. Pile meringue on tops of crabmeat sandwiches. Spread, making swirls in meringue with spatula.
6. Bake in oven at 325°F. for 15 minutes or until delicately browned.

Note

Sandwiches can be made up in individual baking dishes and baked to order.

WESTERN TUNA SANDWICH →

Yield: 1 portion (cooked to order)

Ingredients	
BUTTER or MARGARINE	2 teaspoons
PIMIENTO, chopped	1 tablespoon
GREEN PEPPER, chopped	4 teaspoons
ONION, finely chopped	4 teaspoons
EGG, beaten	1
MILK or WATER	1 tablespoon
SALT	dash
PEPPER	dash
TUNA, drained, flaked	1/4 cup
ROLL, buttered	1

HALIBUT PIMIENTO CHEESE SANDWICH

Yield: 16 portions (2 slices each)

Ingredients	
MAYONNAISE	1 cup
LEMON JUICE	1/3 cup
WORCESTERSHIRE SAUCE	1/4 teaspoon
CAYENNE PEPPER	dash
HALIBUT, cooked, flaked	1 quart
PIMIENTO, chopped	1 cup
SALT	as needed
PEPPER	as needed
BREAD	32 slices
CHEESE, SHARP CHEDDAR, grated	2 pounds

Procedure

1. Mix mayonnaise with lemon juice, Worcestershire, and cayenne.
2. Combine halibut and pimiento. Add dressing; mix lightly but well. Season with salt and pepper.
3. Toast bread on one side.
4. Spread fish mixture in a thin layer on untoasted side. Top each slice with 1/4 cup cheese.
5. Broil until cheese melts, but do not brown. Serve hot.

Procedure

1. Melt butter; add pimiento, green pepper, and onion. Cook over medium heat until vegetables are tender.
2. Combine egg, milk, seasonings, and tuna. Add to vegetable mixture; cook over low heat until egg is set.
3. Serve on buttered roll.

VIENNA SHRIMP BOATS

Yield: 24 sandwiches (1/3 cup filling in each)

Ingredients

SHRIMP, cooked, chopped	1 quart (1-1/2 pounds)
EGGS, hard-cooked, chopped	1-1/2 cups
CELERY, chopped	2 cups
PARSLEY, chopped	1/4 cup
COTTAGE CHEESE, drained	2 cups (1 pound)
LEMON JUICE	1/2 cup
WORCESTERSHIRE SAUCE	1/2 teaspoon
LIQUID HOT PEPPER SEASONING	1/2 teaspoon
SALT	1 teaspoon
MACE	1/4 teaspoon
PAPRIKA	1/4 teaspoon
VIENNA BREAD	2 1-pound loaves
SHRIMP, MEDIUM, WHOLE, cooked	72
GREEN PEPPER STRIPS	48

Procedure

1. Combine shrimp, eggs, celery, and parsley.
2. Combine drained cottage cheese, lemon juice, Worcestershire sauce, hot pepper seasoning, salt, mace, and paprika. Add to shrimp mixture; toss lightly with two forks to blend ingredients.
3. Cut each loaf of bread diagonally into 12 3/4-inch slices.
4. Spread 1/3 cup shrimp salad on each bread slice. Garnish each sandwich with 3 shrimp and 2 green pepper strips.

HOT FISH FLAMINGO SANDWICH

Yield: 25 portions

Ingredients

FISH PORTIONS, FROZEN, RAW, BREADED, 3 OUNCE SIZE	25
SHORTENING, melted or COOKING OIL	1/2 cup
PAPRIKA	1-1/2 teaspoons
CHEESE, grated	1-1/2 pounds
CATSUP	2/3 cup
PREPARED MUSTARD	1/4 cup
HORSERADISH	1/4 cup
BUTTER or MARGARINE	4 ounces
HAMBURGER BUNS, split	25

Procedure

1. Place frozen, raw, breaded fish portions in a single layer in a well-greased baking pan.
2. Pour shortening or oil over fish. Sprinkle with paprika.
3. Bake in oven at 500°F. for 15 to 20 minutes or until fish is browned and flakes easily when tested with a fork.
4. Combine cheese, catsup, mustard, and horseradish.
5. Butter rolls.
6. Place a fish portion on bottom half of each roll. Top with cheese mixture, using a No. 24 scoop.
7. Bake in oven at 350°F. for 8 to 10 minutes or until cheese melts and rolls are thoroughly heated through. Serve hot.

Open Face Tunaburger

Cling Peach Advisory Board

Gourmet Avocado Shrimp Open Face

BARBECUED FISH STICK BUNS ⟶

Yield: 48 portions

Ingredients

BUTTER or MARGARINE	6 ounces
ONION, chopped	1 cup
CELERY, chopped	3 cups
TOMATO SAUCE	1 quart
LEMON JUICE	1 cup
FISH STICKS, 1 OUNCE SIZE	96 (6 pounds)
FRANKFURTER BUNS, sliced	48

GOLDEN GATE TUNA SANDWICH

Yield: 24 sandwiches

Ingredients

TUNA, drained, flaked	1-1/2 quarts
ONION, finely chopped	3/4 cup
CELERY, finely chopped	3/4 cup
OLIVES, RIPE, chopped	3/4 cup
PREPARED MUSTARD	1 tablespoon
MAYONNAISE	3/4 cup
FRANKFURTER ROLLS	24
PIMIENTO CHEESE SPREAD	3 cups
TOMATO PASTE	1 cup
EGGS, hard-cooked, sliced	12
PARSLEY, chopped	as needed

Procedure

1. Flake tuna in large pieces.
2. Combine onion, celery, olives, mustard, and mayonnaise; add to tuna. Mix lightly, but well.
3. Split rolls without cutting all the way through. Fill with tuna mixture.
4. Combine cheese spread and tomato paste; beat until blended.
5. Spoon cheese mixture over tuna. Top with egg slices; sprinkle with parsley.

Procedure

1. Melt butter in a 1-gallon saucepan; add onion and celery, saute until tender.
2. Add tomato sauce and lemon juice, simmer 30 minutes.
3. Heat fish sticks according to package directions.
4. Serve 2 fish sticks and 2 tablespoons sauce in each bun.

SARDINE SUBMARINE SANDWICH

Yield: 2 portions

Ingredients

SUBMARINE ROLL, 12-inch	1
MUSTARD BUTTER*	2 to 3 teaspoons
LETTUCE LEAVES	as needed
TOMATO SLICES	4
ONION SLICES, thin, separated into rings	4
SALT	as needed
CHEESE SLICES, cut diagonally	2
SARDINES, LARGE	4
MUSTARD SAUCE**	3 tablespoons
MAYONNAISE	as needed

Procedure

1. Cut roll in half lengthwise. Spread bottom half with mustard butter. Cover with lettuce leaves.
2. Arrange tomato slices and onion rings on top of lettuce. Sprinkle with salt. Cover with triangles of cheese. Lay sardines crosswise on top.
3. Pour mustard sauce over sardines.
4. Spread top portion of roll with mayonnaise. Cover sandwich, securing with wooden picks. Cut across into 2 portions.

*To make mustard butter: blend 8 ounces softened butter with 1/4 cup prepared mustard. Makes enough to spread 24 rolls or 48 sandwiches.

**To make mustard sauce: combine 1 quart mayonnaise with 1 cup prepared mustard, 1/3 cup pickle juice, and a few dashes of hot liquid pepper seasoning. Makes enough for 24 rolls or 48 sandwiches.

SEA SPECIAL SANDWICH

Yield: 24 sandwiches

Ingredients	
BUNS, ROUND, SEEDED, SOFT, split	24
LETTUCE LEAVES	24
TOMATO SLICES	24
FISH PORTIONS, BREADED, deep fried	24
MAYONNAISE	3/4 cup
SOUR CREAM	3/4 cup
CHEESE, BLEU, crumbled	2 ounces
BACON, cooked	24 strips

CRABMEAT-PINEAPPLE CLUB SANDWICH

Yield: 50 sandwiches

Ingredients	
PINEAPPLE TIDBITS, drained	1 No. 10 can
CRABMEAT	3 quarts
CELERY, finely chopped	1-1/2 quarts
GREEN ONIONS, finely chopped	1-1/2 cups
MAYONNAISE	1-1/2 cups
TOAST, buttered	150 slices
BACON, cooked, crisp	100 slices
TOMATO, FIRM RIPE	100 slices
CHERRY TOMATOES	as needed
PINEAPPLE TIDBITS	as needed

Procedure

1. Combine drained pineapple with crabmeat, celery, green onions, and mayonnaise.
2. Make sandwiches 3-decker style, using 3 pieces of toast for each. Use bacon and tomato slices for bottom layer, fill top layer with crabmeat mixture.
3. Skewer cherry tomatoes and additional pineapple tidbits on picks for garnish, if desired. Stick into top of sandwich.

Procedure

1. Open buns. Place a lettuce leaf, then a tomato slice, on bottom portion of each bun.
2. Place hot fish portions on top of tomato slices.
3. Combine mayonnaise, sour cream, and cheese. Top fish with cheese mixture allowing about 1/2 ounce per portion.
4. Add bacon strips. Cover with top sections of buns.

Note

Use 1-1/2 cups bottled bleu cheese dressing in place of mayonnaise, sour cream, and cheese, if desired.

SHRIMP SOUFFLE SANDWICH

Yield: 48 portions

Ingredients

ENRICHED BREAD, day-old	96 slices
SHRIMP, cooked, finely chopped	3 quarts
CELERY, chopped	3 cups
GREEN PEPPER, chopped	3 cups
CHEESE, AMERICAN, grated	1-1/2 pounds
NONFAT DRY MILK	1 pound
WATER	1 gallon
EGGS, beaten	3 pounds, 12 ounces
SALT	1/4 cup
PAPRIKA	1 tablespoon

Procedure

1. Arrange 8 bread slices in each of 6 greased 11-inch by 16-inch by 2-1/2-inch pans.
2. Combine shrimp, celery, and green pepper. Spread a No. 16 scoop of shrimp mixture over each bread slice in pan. Sprinkle with cheese. Cover with remaining bread slices, making sandwiches.
3. Sift dry milk over water; beat to blend. Add eggs and salt; blend.
4. Pour custard mixture over sandwiches, allowing about 1 quart per pan. Sprinkle with paprika.
5. Bake in oven at 350°F. for about 45 minutes.

TOASTED MAINE SARDINE-CHEESE SANDWICH →

Yield: 100 sandwiches

Ingredients

SARDINES	10 12-ounce cans
BUTTER or MARGARINE, softened	1 pound
PREPARED MUSTARD	1/3 cup
BREAD SLICES	100
CHEESE, 1-ounce slices	100
PAPRIKA	as needed

DEVILED LOBSTER SANDWICH

Yield: 48 sandwiches, 3 quarts filling

Ingredients

LOBSTER, cooked, flaked	3 pounds, 12 ounces
CELERY, finely chopped	1-1/2 pounds
ONION, grated	2 tablespoons
PREPARED MUSTARD	2 tablespoons
WORCESTERSHIRE SAUCE	1/4 cup
MAYONNAISE	1 quart
SALT	as needed
WHITE PEPPER	as needed
BUTTER or MARGARINE	1-1/2 pounds
VIENNA BREAD	96 slices

Procedure

1. Combine lobster, celery, onion, mustard, Worcestershire sauce, and mayonnaise. Season with salt and pepper.

2. Spread bread slices with butter or margarine. Make into sandwiches, allowing No. 16 scoop of filling per sandwich. Cut in desired shape; garnish with watercress.

Procedure

1. Drain sardines.
2. Combine butter and mustard; mix well. Spread bread. Place in a single layer on sheetpans.
3. Arrange sardines on bread; cover with cheese. Sprinkle with paprika. Top with additional whole sardines, if desired.
4. Toast in oven at 450°F. for 8 to 10 minutes or until cheese melts and bread toasts. Serve hot.

FISH STICK-CHEESE BURGERS

Yield: 100 burgers

Ingredients

FISH STICKS, 1-OUNCE	200
BUTTER or MARGARINE, softened	1 pound
HAMBURGER ROLLS	100
CHILI SAUCE	1-1/2 quarts
CHEESE, 1-ounce slices	100

Procedure

1. Place frozen fish sticks in single layer in well-greased baking pans. Bake in oven at 400°F. for 15 to 20 minutes or until heated through.
2. Spread butter on rolls.
3. Arrange 2 fish sticks on bottom half of each roll. Top with about 1 tablespoon chili sauce, a slice of cheese, and top half of roll.
4. Bake in oven at 350°F. for 8 to 10 minutes or until cheese melts. Serve hot.

FISH HERO SANDWICH

Yield: 24 portions

Ingredients

FRENCH or ALL-PURPOSE SANDWICH ROLLS	24 (3-inches by 6-1/2-inches)
CABBAGE, shredded	1-1/2 pounds
RIPE OLIVE SLAW DRESSING*	1-1/2 quarts
FISH, FROZEN, BREADED, prepared according to package directions	24 2-ounce portions
TOMATOES, SMALL, cut into thin slices	1-1/2 pounds
OLIVES, RIPE, WHOLE	24
LEMON WEDGES, small	24
PARSLEY SPRIGS, small	24

Procedure

1. Split rolls; toast.
2. Combine cabbage with 3 cups Ripe Olive Slaw Dressing.*
3. For each portion, spread 2 ounces slaw on bottom half of roll. Top slaw with 1 portion hot breaded fish. Spread top half roll with 1 ounce of remaining dressing; cover with 1 ounce of tomato slices.
4. Garnish each portion with ripe olive, lemon wedge, parsley sprig.

*RIPE OLIVE SLAW DRESSING

Yield: 1-1/2 quarts

Ingredients

MAYONNAISE	1 pound, 2 ounces (1 quart)
VINEGAR	1/3 cup
PREPARED HORSERADISH	2-1/2 tablespoons
PREPARED MUSTARD	2-1/2 tablespoons
ONION POWDER	2 teaspoons
SALT	2 teaspoons
OLIVES, RIPE, SLICED, well drained	10 ounces (2-1/2 cups)
PIMIENTO, chopped	4 ounces (1/2 cup)

Procedure

1. Combine mayonnaise, vinegar, horseradish, mustard, onion powder, and salt; mix thoroughly.
2. Add well-drained olives and pimiento; mix to distribute evenly.

FRENCH-TOASTED TUNA SANDWICH

Yield: 50 portions

Ingredients

TUNA, flaked	8 6-1/2-ounce cans
CELERY, chopped	1 quart
SWEET PICKLES, chopped	2 cups
SALAD DRESSING	2 cups
BREAD	100 slices
EGGS, slightly beaten	24
MILK	3 cups
SALT	2 teaspoons

Procedure

1. Combine tuna, celery, chopped pickles, and salad dressing.
2. Spread 1/4 cup mixture on 50 slices of bread. Cover with remaining bread slices.
3. Blend eggs, milk, and salt. Dip sandwiches in mixture; brown slowly on both sides in well-buttered skillet or on griddle.

TOASTED BUNS WITH CRABMEAT AND CHEESE

Yield: 32 portions

Ingredients

CRABMEAT	5 6-1/2-ounce cans
CELERY, finely diced	1 cup
SWEET PICKLE, minced	1 cup
MAYONNAISE	2 cups
BUNS, cut in half	32
BUTTER or MARGARINE	5 ounces
CHEESE, AMERICAN, sliced	32 3/4-ounce slices
or CHEESE, AMERICAN, grated	1-1/2 pounds

Procedure

1. Drain crabmeat. Remove any shell or cartilage; flake.
2. Combine crabmeat, celery, pickle, and mayonnaise. Spread on bottom halves of buns.
3. Butter top halves of buns; toast. Cover with cheese. Heat under broiler until cheese is soft.
4. Serve one cheese half and one crabmeat half as an open-faced sandwich.

HOT SHRIMP SALAD SANDWICH →

Yield: 30 sandwiches

Ingredients

SHRIMP, cooked, cleaned, cut up	2-1/2 pounds (ready-to-use weight)
FRENCH DRESSING	1/3 cup
CELERY, finely diced	3 cups
MAYONNAISE	as needed
SALT	1 teaspoon
WHITE BREAD	30 slices
CHEESE, PROCESS AMERICAN	30 1-ounce slices

SHRIMP SALAD SANDWICH

Yield: 24 sandwiches

Ingredients

CREAM CHEESE	8 ounces
SOUR CREAM	1 cup
LEMON JUICE	2 tablespoons
CHIVES, finely cut	1/4 cup
GREEN PEPPER, finely chopped	1 cup
OLIVES, RIPE, SLICED	1-1/2 cups
MUSHROOMS, CANNED, chopped	1-1/2 cups
SHRIMP, WHOLE, VERY SMALL, cooked	1-1/4 quarts
SALT	as needed
WHITE PEPPER	as needed
WHITE BREAD	24 slices
WHOLE WHEAT BREAD	24 slices

Procedure

1. Blend cream cheese and sour cream.
2. Add lemon juice, chives, green pepper, olives, mushrooms, and shrimp. Season with salt and pepper.
3. Spread white bread with salad mixture; cover with whole wheat bread.
4. Cut sandwiches diagonally into thirds. Place on serving plate, inverting middle section so white bread is on top.

Procedure

1. Marinate the shrimp in french dressing for at least 30 minutes, stirring frequently.
2. Combine shrimp and celery; add mayonnaise to moisten. Add salt.
3. Spread the shrimp filling on slices of bread; cover each with a slice of cheese. Place under broiler until the cheese is melted and slightly brown.

GRILLED SALMON SANDWICH

Yield: 24 sandwiches

Ingredients

SALMON, CANNED, drained, flaked	3 cups
CHEESE, CHEDDAR, shredded	1-1/2 pounds
EGGS, hard-cooked, chopped	4
GREEN PEPPER, chopped	1/2 cup
SWEET RELISH	1/3 cup
SALAD DRESSING	1/2 cup
PREPARED MUSTARD	3 tablespoons
SALT	1/2 teaspoon
PEPPER	1/2 teaspoon
BREAD	48 slices
BUTTER or MARGARINE, softened	as needed

Procedure

1. Combine salmon, cheese, eggs, green pepper, relish, salad dressing, mustard, salt, and pepper. Refrigerate 1 hour.
2. Make up sandwiches allowing a No. 16 scoop of filling for each.
3. Brush outside surfaces of sandwiches with butter. Grill on both sides until filling is hot and sandwiches are golden brown.

RIPE OLIVE TUNA PUFF SANDWICH

Yield: 25 sandwiches

Ingredients

FILLING	
TUNA, drained, flaked	5 12-1/2-ounce cans
OLIVES, RIPE, CHOPPED, drained	2-1/2 cups
CELERY, finely chopped	2-1/2 cups
ONION, finely chopped	2/3 cup
PARSLEY, finely chopped	1/2 cup
SAVORY, CRUMBLED	2 teaspoons
MAYONNAISE	1-3/4 cups
TOPPING	
MAYONNAISE	3 cups
OLIVES, RIPE, drained, chopped	3/4 cup
CHEESE, PARMESAN, grated	3/4 cup
BAKING POWDER	1 tablespoon
RYE BREAD	50 slices

Procedure

1. For filling, combine tuna, first amount of ripe olives, celery, onion, parsley, savory, and first amount of mayonnaise; toss together until well mixed.

2. For topping, beat second amount of mayonnaise with rotary beater. Fold in remaining olives, parmesan cheese, and baking powder.

3. To assemble sandwiches, toast bread, on one side, under broiler. Turn slices. Spread each slice with a No. 20 scoop of the tuna filling. Portion a No. 60 scoop of topping on each slice; spread. Broil until topping bubbles and browns. Stack 2 slices, filling side up, for each sandwich.

Sandwich Fillings

ALMOND-SALMON SANDWICH FILLING

Yield: 2-1/2 quarts

Ingredients

ALMONDS, ROASTED, diced	3-3/4 cups
SALMON, CANNED or cooked	1-1/4 quarts
LEMON JUICE	1/3 cup
CELERY SALT	2-1/2 teaspoons
MAYONNAISE	2 cups
PICKLE RELISH	1-1/4 cups

Procedure

Combine ingredients; blend thoroughly. Refrigerate.

DEVILED CLAM SANDWICH FILLING

Yield: 1 quart

Ingredients

MAYONNAISE or SALAD DRESSING	1/2 cup
DRY MUSTARD	1-1/2 teaspoons
SALT	1-1/2 teaspoons
PEPPER	1/4 teaspoon
CHIVES, chopped	1-1/2 tablespoons
CELERY, chopped	1/2 cup
EGGS, hard-cooked, sieved	3 cups
CLAMS, cooked, drained, minced	2-1/2 cups

Procedure

1. Combine mayonnaise, mustard, salt, pepper, and chives.
2. Add celery, sieved egg, and minced clams; mix.

DILLY SHRIMP-CUCUMBER SANDWICH FILLING ➛

Yield: 1 quart

Ingredients

LEMON JUICE	2 tablespoons
SALT	1/2 teaspoon
CREAM CHEESE	1 pound
DILL SEED	1 teaspoon
CUCUMBER, unpeeled, chopped	1-1/3 cups
SHRIMP, cooked, chopped	1-1/3 cups

CRABMEAT-EGG SANDWICH FILLING

Yield: 1 gallon

Ingredients

CRABMEAT, FRESH, FROZEN or CANNED, flaked	2 quarts, 1/2 cup*
EGGS, hard-cooked, chopped	2 quarts
CELERY SALT	2-1/2 tablespoons
LEMON JUICE	2-1/2 tablespoons
PIMIENTO, chopped	1 cup
MAYONNAISE or SALAD DRESSING	2 cups

*Equivalent to four 13-ounce cans

Procedure

Combine ingredients; mix well. Chill.

Procedure

1. Blend lemon juice and salt with cream cheese.
2. Add dill seed, cucumber, and shrimp; mix.

Note

Flavor combines well with rye bread.

TUNA SALAD SANDWICH FILLING

Yield: approximately 1 quart

Ingredients

TUNA, drained, flaked	1 pound
PICKLES, SWEET or DILL, chopped	1-1/2 cups
CELERY, chopped	3/4 cup
MAYONNAISE or SALAD DRESSING	1/2 cup
LEMON JUICE	2 tablespoons
SALT	3/4 teaspoon
PEPPER	1/4 teaspoon

Procedure

1. Combine ingredients; mix well. Chill.
2. Use with white, whole wheat, or egg twist bread.

Cheese-Topped Sandwich with Seafood Filling

Wheat Flour Institute

Salads

Few Calories in Salad Supreme

Cling Peach Advisory Board; California Blue Diamond Almond Growers Exchange

Low Calory Deep Sea Salad

General Foods Corp., Institutional Food Service Division; Cling Peach Advisory Board

CRAB LOUIS

Yield: 1 portion

Ingredients

LETTUCE LEAVES	as needed
LETTUCE, ICEBERG, shredded	1/2 cup
KING CRABMEAT, chunks	3 ounces
CUCUMBER SLICES	3
OLIVES, RIPE, LARGE	2
EGGS, hard-cooked quarters	2
CRAB LOUIS DRESSING*	1/4 cup

Procedure

1. Line shallow salad bowl with lettuce leaves; mound shredded lettuce in center.
2. Arrange crabmeat on top, cucumber slices, ripe olives, and egg quarters at the side.
3. Drizzle with dressing.

*CRAB LOUIS DRESSING

Yield: 1-1/2 quarts

Ingredients

MAYONNAISE	3 cups
CREAM, HEAVY	3/4 cup
CHILI SAUCE	3/4 cup
WORCESTERSHIRE SAUCE	1 tablespoon
GREEN PEPPER, minced	3/4 cup
ONION, minced	3/4 cup
LEMON JUICE	1/3 cup

Procedure

Combine ingredients; chill.

ALASKA KING CRAB A L'OPERA WITH ROSSINI DRESSING →

Yield: 32 portions

Ingredients	
WINE VINEGAR	3/4 cup
LEMON JUICE	1/4 cup
DRY MUSTARD	1 tablespoon
WHITE PEPPER	1 teaspoon
SALT	1 tablespoon
OLIVE OIL	3 cups
TRUFFLES, chopped	3 tablespoons
KING CRABMEAT and LEGS	6 pounds
CELERY, cut julienne	2 pounds, 10 ounces
TOMATOES, WHOLE, peeled, chilled	32
LETTUCE	as needed

SALMON PLATE ESPERANTO

Yield: 24 portions

Ingredients	
SALMON STEAKS, 5-OUNCE	24
OLIVES, GREEN, PIMIENTO-STUFFED, chopped	1 cup
TARTAR SAUCE	1-1/4 quarts
LETTUCE, ICEBERG, separated as leaves	as needed
GERMAN POTATO SALAD,* hot or cold	3 quarts
TOMATO SLICES	72
CUCUMBER SLICES	72
DILL WEED	as needed
LEMON WEDGES	48
PARSLEY SPRIGS	24

Procedure

1. Poach salmon; drain. Chill.
2. Combine olives and tartar sauce.
3. For each portion, line plate with crisp lettuce. Arrange salmon on lettuce, top with olive tartar sauce. Portion 1/2 cup potato salad on plate. Alternate slices of cucumber and tomato; sprinkle with dill weed. Garnish with lemon wedges and parsley.

---

*See recipe, facing page

Procedure

1. Combine vinegar, lemon juice, mustard, pepper, and salt. Mix to dissolve salt. Add oil; blend. Add truffles.

2. Combine crabmeat and celery, reserving 32 slices of crab leg for garnish. Add dressing. Refrigerate to marinate at least 30 minutes.

3. Cut each tomato into eighths, from the bottom to 3/4 inch from the stem end; press sections outward to form a petaled shape.

4. Place tomatoes on a chilled lettuce bed. Fill tomato with crab mixture. Garnish with the reserved crab legs.

*GERMAN POTATO SALAD

Yield: 30 portions

Ingredients

BACON, RAW, diced	1 pound
CELERY, finely diced	1 pound
ONION finely chopped	12 ounces
GREEN PEPPER, finely diced	4 ounces
FLOUR	5 to 6 tablespoons
VINEGAR, hot	2 cups
STOCK or WATER, hot	3 to 4 cups
SUGAR	4 ounces
PEPPER	1 teaspoon
SALT	as needed
POTATOES, FROZEN, SLICED	8 pounds

Procedure

1. Fry bacon until crisp. Add celery, onion, and green pepper; saute very lightly.

2. Add just enough flour to pick up excess bacon fat; cook 2 to 3 minutes.

3. Add hot vinegar and stock gradually. Cook and stir until smooth and thickened to consistency of heavy cream. Add sugar and pepper. Adjust consistency, if necessary. Check seasoning, add salt as needed.

4. Place frozen sliced potatoes in 12-inch by 20-inch steam table pan. Pour hot dressing over potatoes; mix to coat potatoes. Cover pan tightly with foil.

5. Bake in oven at 450°F. for 50 minutes.

TOMATO AND SARDINE PLATE

Yield: 1 portion

Ingredients

LETTUCE LEAVES	as needed
LETTUCE, shredded, marinated	3 ounces
TOMATO SLICES	5
SARDINES	2 ounces
EGG, hard-cooked, sliced	1
FRENCH DRESSING	2 tablespoons
PARSLEY	sprig

Procedure

1. Line 8-inch plate with lettuce leaves. Place 3 ounces marinated shredded lettuce in center of plate.
2. Arrange 5 tomato slices in a circle.
3. Arrange 2 ounces sardines in the center of the circle.
4. Arrange slices of 1 egg around sardines.
5. Pour 2 tablespoons french dressing over salad. Garnish with parsley sprig.

MONTPELIER SALAD

Yield: 4 portions

Ingredients

LETTUCE, BOSTON, shredded	2 heads
CRABMEAT, FRESH, LUMP	1/2 pound
SHRIMP, cooked, split in half	10
CHEESE, SWISS, cut julienne	10 ounces
RADISHES, RED	4
EGGS, hard-cooked, quartered	2
ASPARAGUS TIPS	4
TOMATOES	4 slices

Procedure

1. Arrange lettuce on bottom of a large salad bowl.
2. Arrange crabmeat, shrimp, and cheese on lettuce. Garnish with radishes, eggs, asparagus, and tomatoes, making a colorful, artistic arrangement.
3. Serve with french dressing.

SHRIMP-STUFFED ARTICHOKES

Yield: 48 portions

Ingredients

CONCORD GRAPE JAM or JELLY	1 cup (10 ounces)
LEMON JUICE	1/2 cup
SOUR CREAM	2-3/4 quarts
HORSERADISH	1 cup
DRY MUSTARD	1/4 cup
MAYONNAISE	3 cups
CATSUP	1-1/2 cups
ONION JUICE	1-1/3 cups
ARTICHOKES, LARGE	48
WATER, salted	as needed
LEMON JUICE	1 cup
SHRIMP, CANNED, TINY COCKTAIL, undrained	9 pounds
PARSLEY, chopped	as needed

Procedure

1. Combine jam, lemon juice, sour cream, horseradish, mustard, mayonnaise, catsup, and onion juice; stir until blended. Chill until ready to use.
2. Wash artichokes; drain. Cut off stem so artichoke will sit level. Remove tough bottom leaves. With heavy knife, cut about one inch off top of artichoke. With shears, trim off thorny tip of each leaf.
3. Place in a pan with one to two inches of salted water. Add lemon juice. Cover; cook until fork tender, about 45 minutes. Drain. Chill.
4. Gently force artichoke leaves apart; insert a melon ball cutter into the center; rotate to scoop out the "choke" of each.
5. Drain shrimp thoroughly.
6. Divide chilled sauce into two equal parts. Pour one part over drained shrimp; mix gently.
7. Spoon mixture into centers of artichokes. Arrange on crisp salad greens.
8. Portion remaining sauce into souffle cups or fluted lemon cups. Sprinkle with chopped parsley; place beside artichokes to be used as a dip for the leaves.
9. Garnish plates with ripe olives and wedges of tomato, hard-cooked eggs, and lemon, as desired.

HOT SEAFOOD 'N CHEESE SALAD →

Yield: 24 portions

Ingredients

SHRIMP, cooked, diced	2 quarts
CHEESE, BRICK, cubed	2 quarts
CELERY, chopped	1 quart
ALMONDS, SLIVERED, toasted	1 cup
GREEN PEPPER, chopped	1 cup
SOUR CREAM	1 quart
CHEESE, BLUE, crumbled	1 cup
ONION, minced	1/2 cup
LEMON JUICE	1 cup
SALT	1 tablespoon
CORN FLAKE CRUMBS	2 cups
BUTTER, melted	1/2 cup
CHEESE, BLUE, crumbled	as needed

TUNA MOUSSE

Yield: 24 portions

Ingredients

GELATINE, UNFLAVORED	3 tablespoons
WATER, cold	3/4 cup
MAYONNAISE	1 quart
TUNA, finely flaked	6 6-ounce cans
EGGS, hard-cooked, chopped	6
OLIVES, GREEN, STUFFED, chopped	1-1/2 cups
CAPERS	6 tablespoons
CHIVES, chopped or ONION, minced	3 tablespoons

Procedure

1. Soften gelatine in cold water; dissolve over hot water.
2. Stir in mayonnaise.
3. Combine remaining ingredients; fold into mayonnaise mixture.
4. Turn into a 10-inch by 12-inch by 2-1/2-inch pan or individual molds. Chill until firm.
5. Serve on crisp salad greens. Garnish with mayonnaise, parsley, and stuffed olives.

Procedure

1. Combine shrimp, brick cheese, celery, almonds, and green pepper; toss lightly to mix.
2. Blend sour cream, first amount of blue cheese, onion, lemon juice, and salt. Pour over shrimp mixture; toss lightly to mix.
3. Portion mixture into individual baking shells or ramekins allowing about 1 cup mixture per shell.
4. Combine corn flake crumbs and melted butter; sprinkle over tops.
5. Bake in oven at 300°F. for 10 to 15 minutes or until just heated. Top with additional crumbled blue cheese.

AVOCADO SEAFOOD SALAD

Yield: 16 portions

Ingredients

LOBSTER TAILS, boiled	16
AVOCADOS, cut in large chunks	8
CHIVES or ONION, finely chopped	1/4 cup
LEMON JUICE	2 tablespoons
CHILI POWDER	2 teaspoons
MAYONNAISE	1-1/2 cups
SALT	as needed
AVOCADOS, cut in rings	as needed
LEMON JUICE	as needed
LEMON WEDGES	as needed

Procedure

1. Remove meat from lobster tails, reserving shells. Dice meat.
2. Combine lobster meat with avocado chunks.
3. Combine chives, first amount of lemon juice, chili powder, and mayonnaise; blend. Season with salt. Add dressing to lobster mixture; toss lightly to mix.
4. Spoon mixture into lobster tail shells. Serve on greens. Garnish with avocado rings (which have been dipped in lemon juice) and lemon wedges.

Note

If desired, pile diced lobster and avocado in shells. Serve dressing separately.

SHRIMP SALAD BOWL WITH REMOULADE SAUCE

Yield: 16 portions

Ingredients

SHRIMP, LARGE or JUMBO, FRESH or FROZEN	5 pounds
or SHRIMP, FROZEN, SHELLED, DEVEINED	3 pounds
SALT	1/4 cup
PICKLING SPICES	2 teaspoons
LEAF LETTUCE, CURLY ENDIVE, and ESCAROLE, cleaned, torn into pieces	1-1/2 gallons
EGGS, hard-cooked, cut in quarters	1 dozen
TOMATOES, cut in wedges	6 to 8
OLIVES, RIPE	48

Procedure

1. Cook shrimp 3 to 5 minutes in boiling water with salt and pickling spices.
2. Drain, shell and devein shrimp; chill.
3. Put 1-1/2 cups prepared salad greens in individual salad bowl. Arrange 6 to 8 shrimp across half of greens; arrange 3 wedges of egg and 3 tomato wedges on remaining half. Center with 3 ripe olives.
4. Top with 1/4 cup Remoulade Sauce or, serve sauce separately.

REMOULADE SAUCE

Yield: approximately 1 quart

Ingredients

MAYONNAISE	3-1/2 cups
GARLIC, crushed	2 cloves
DRY MUSTARD	1 tablespoon
TARRAGON, DRY	3/4 teaspoon
PARSLEY, minced	1/4 cup
PICKLES, SOUR, finely chopped	1/2 cup
CAPERS, chopped	1-1/2 tablespoons

Procedure

Combine all ingredients, mixing thoroughly. Let stand, in refrigerator, for at least 1/2 hour to blend flavors. Serve cold.

DILLED SHRIMP SALAD

Yield: 24 3/4-cup portions

Ingredients

SHRIMP, cooked, cleaned	4 pounds
CELERY, thinly sliced	1-1/2 pounds
SALAD OIL	2/3 cup
WINE VINEGAR	1/3 cup
DILL WEED	2 teaspoons
SALT	1 teaspoon
WHITE PEPPER	1/4 teaspoon
LIQUID HOT PEPPER SEASONING	few drops

Procedure

1. Place shrimp and celery in mixing bowl.
2. Combine remaining ingredients; mix well. Pour over shrimp mixture; toss lightly.
3. Chill thoroughly. Serve on crisp salad greens.

OLIVE AND TUNA LOAF

Yield: 1 gallon, 32 1/2-cup portions

Ingredients

GELATIN, LEMON FLAVOR	24 ounces
WATER, boiling	1-1/2 quarts
WATER, cold	1-1/4 quarts
VINEGAR	1/2 cup
CELERY, chopped	1 cup
ONION, finely chopped	1 cup
WALNUTS, chopped	1 cup
OLIVES, PIMIENTO-STUFFED, sliced	3 cups
TUNA, CANNED, flaked	14 ounces

Procedure

1. Dissolve gelatin in boiling water; add cold water and vinegar. Chill until slightly thickened.
2. Combine remaining ingredients; toss gently to mix. Fold into gelatin mixture.
3. Pour into loaf pans. Chill until firm.
4. Unmold onto salad greens. Serve with mayonnaise.

PEAR AND TUNA SALAD

Yield: 50 portions

Ingredients

LETTUCE, ICEBERG	4 heads
PEARS, FRESH	25 (8 to 9 pounds)
LEMON JUICE	as needed
TUNA	8 pounds
CELERY, chopped	3 quarts
ONION SALT	1 teaspoon
SALT	2 tablespoons
WHITE PEPPER	1/2 teaspoon
FRENCH DRESSING	1/2 cup
MAYONNAISE	1 quart
LEMON JUICE	2 tablespoons
EGGS, hard-cooked, chopped	12
TOMATOES, cut in wedges	8 pounds
PARSLEY, sprigs	50

Procedure

1. Wash lettuce, remove core, separate leaves, and refrigerate until needed.

2. Wash pears, cut in half. Remove stem; core and scoop out center. Rub with lemon.

3. Drain tuna. Place in a large bowl; flake.

4. Combine celery, onion salt, salt, white pepper, french dressing, mayonnaise, lemon juice, and hard-cooked eggs; add to tuna. Mix lightly.

5. To serve, arrange a pear half on lettuce, placing cut side up; place a No. 12 scoop of tuna salad on pear. Garnish with tomato wedges and a sprig of parsley. Serve as a cold plate with potato salad and coleslaw, if desired.

Seafood Fruit Plate

California Prune Advisory Board

Fisherman's Salad

Spanish Green Olive Commission

SHRIMP MACARONI SALAD →

Yield: 30 portions

Ingredients

MACARONI, ELBOW or SHELLS	1-1/2 pounds
FRENCH DRESSING	1 cup
SALT	1-1/2 tablespoons
PAPRIKA	1 teaspoon
CELERY, chopped	1 quart
GREEN PEPPER, chopped	1 cup
PIMIENTO, chopped	1 cup
ONION, ground or grated	1 cup
SHRIMP, cooked, peeled, cut into pieces	1-1/2 pounds (ready-to-use weight)
MAYONNAISE	1 quart

ROCK LOBSTER AND POTATO SALAD

Yield: 25 portions

Ingredients

SOUTH AFRICAN ROCK LOBSTER TAILS	10 pounds
POTATOES, MEDIUM, unpeeled	12 pounds
OLIVE OIL	1-1/2 cups
TARRAGON VINEGAR	1-1/2 cups
TARTAR SAUCE or MAYONNAISE	2 tablespoons
OLIVES, PIMIENTO-STUFFED, finely chopped	1/2 cup
SALT	2 tablespoons
ONION, finely chopped	1 cup

Procedure

1. Drop frozen rock lobster tails in boiling salted water. Bring water back to a boil; cook lobster tails until just done. (Figure time in minutes by weight of individual tails plus 3. For example, 4-ounce tails cook in 7 minutes.) Remove tails, reserving water.
2. Cool lobster; remove from shells. Dice.
3. Cook potatoes in rock lobster water until done. Peel and slice potatoes while hot.
4. Mix olive oil, vinegar, tartar sauce, olives, and salt. Pour over warm potatoes; mix lightly.
5. Mix in lobster and onion. Chill thoroughly. Serve on crisp salad greens. Garnish with avocado squares and strips of pimiento, if desired.

Procedure

1. Cook macaroni according to package directions; drain.
2. Combine french dressing, salt, and paprika; pour over the hot macaroni. Toss to mix. Allow to cool.
3. Combine marinated macaroni with remaining ingredients; toss lightly to mix.
4. Serve on crisp salad greens. Garnish with parsley and hard-cooked egg, if desired.

OLIVE-TUNA STUFFED AVOCADOS

Yield: 24 portions

Ingredients

TUNA	26 ounces
CELERY, finely chopped	6 ounces
ONION, finely chopped	1/2 cup
OLIVES, RIPE, chopped	2 cups
MAYONNAISE	3/4 cup
PREPARED MUSTARD	2 teaspoons
WHITE PEPPER	1/4 teaspoon
AVOCADOS, SMALL	12
LEMON JUICE	1/4 cup
PIMIENTO STRIPS	24
LETTUCE	as needed

Procedure

1. Drain tuna; flake.
2. Add celery, onion, and olives.
3. Combine mayonnaise, mustard, and pepper; blend with tuna mixture.
4. Cut avocados into halves; remove seeds and skins. Sprinkle halves with lemon juice to prevent darkening.
5. Fill avocado halves with tuna mixture, using No. 24 scoop. Garnish with pimiento strip. Arrange on lettuce.

SALMON SALAD

Yield: 25 1/2-cup portions

Ingredients	
MAYONNAISE	2 cups
LEMON JUICE	2 tablespoons
PREPARED MUSTARD	1-1/2 teaspoons
SALT	1 tablespoon
PICKLES, SWEET, chopped	1-1/2 cups
ONION, finely chopped	2 tablespoons
PIMIENTO, diced	1/4 cup
EGGS, hard-cooked, chopped	6
CELERY, chopped	1-1/4 quarts
SALMON, drained, cleaned, flaked	5 1-pound cans

Procedure

1. Combine mayonnaise, lemon juice, mustard, salt, pickles, onion, pimiento, eggs, and celery.
2. Remove skin and large bones from drained salmon; flake in fairly large pieces. Add to mayonnaise mixture.
3. Toss lightly to mix. Chill.
4. Serve in lettuce cups. If desired, place 1/3 cup shredded iceberg lettuce in bottom of lettuce cup; arrange the salmon salad on top.

Note

2-1/2 quarts of flaked tuna, crabmeat, or cooked white-fleshed fish may be substituted for salmon.

TUNA MOLD

Yield: 3 large (1-1/2 quarts each) molds or 36 4-ounce molds

Ingredients

TUNA, flaked	6 6-1/2-ounce cans
EGGS, hard-cooked, chopped	9
OLIVES, GREEN, STUFFED, sliced	1-1/2 cups
CAPERS	6 tablespoons
ONION, minced	3 tablespoons
GELATINE, UNFLAVORED	1-1/2 ounces
WATER, cold	3/4 cup
MAYONNAISE	1-1/2 quarts

Procedure

1. Combine tuna, eggs, olives, capers, and onion.
2. Soften gelatine in cold water for 5 minutes. Dissolve over hot water.
3. Add dissolved gelatine to mayonnaise, stirring constantly.
4. Add mayonnaise mixture to tuna mixture; mix thoroughly.
5. Pour into molds; chill until firm.
6. Unmold on lettuce or chicory. Garnish with deviled eggs, tomato, or avocado wedges, if desired.

Note

To decorate large fish molds, cut ripe olives into thin wedges and lay in a row along the back to simulate fins; use two slices of stuffed olives as eyes, and arrange strips of pimiento to suggest a fish tail.

Tomato Stuffed with Shrimp-Vegetable Salad

McIlhenny Company, manufacturers of Tabasco products

Serving Suggestions for Breaded Fish Sticks or Fried Portions

Serve with a companionable sauce as, for example:
- Tartar Sauce
- Tomato Sauce
- Spanish Sauce
- Chili Sauce or Catsup
- Sweet-Sour Sauce
- A well-seasoned Cream Sauce combined with:
  - Parsley
  - Pimiento
  - Finely chopped hard-cooked egg
  - Sliced mushrooms
  - Blanched green pepper shreds
  - Cooked celery slices
  - Baby shrimp
- Mayonnaise seasoned with curry powder
- Mayonnaise combined with chopped chives or a hint of onion and diced cucumber, crumbled bleu cheese or chopped fresh dill

Accompany with crisp bacon strips and halved cherry tomatoes

Serve on french-style green beans flecked with bits of pimiento; top with mornay sauce

Combine with breaded scallops and shrimp for a mixed fry

Top with creamed eggs or vegetables a la king

Sprinkle with grated sharp cheese and finish by heating in the oven

Accompany with lyonnaise potatoes and a few slices of pickled beets

Feature with baked beans and an old-fashioned cabbage salad

Offer with au gratin or escalloped potatoes or with creamed, whole new potatoes and peas

Present as a sandwich on a soft bun topped with sliced tomato and shredded lettuce or cabbage slaw

Garnish with a small mold of tomato aspic
Bill with hot potato salad, spaghetti in tomato sauce, spanish rice, or macaroni and cheese
Accompany with mustard pickles, corn relish, whole cranberry sauce, three-bean salad, or dilled peach halves
Serve on a bed of chopped broccoli; top with small white onions in a smooth cheese sauce
Top with zesty Orange Sauce; present with scrambled eggs.
Team with rice and mushroom chow mein

From lower left, up and down: Country French Fish and Fries; Haddock Hawaiian (with fruit-rice salad in shell); Fish Portions Paesan; Seaman's Special; Fish on Rye (fish portions, Swiss cheese, cole slaw)

National Fisheries Institute

Fish and Chips American Style (top); Wikiwiki I'A, Fish Portions with Sweet and Sour Sauce (bottom)

National Fisheries Institute

Canned, Cooked, Dried Fish Entrees

BAKED SHRIMP AND TUNA NEWBURG

Yield: 50 3/4-cup portions

Ingredients

BUTTER or MARGARINE	1 pound
FLOUR	3 cups (12 ounces)
CREAM, LIGHT	1 gallon
SALT	2 teaspoons
LIQUID HOT PEPPER SEASONING	1/2 teaspoon
WORCESTERSHIRE SAUCE	2 tablespoons
SHERRY WINE	1 cup
FISH, flaked	6 7-ounce cans
SHRIMP, drained	4 5- to 7-ounce cans
TUNA in OIL, flaked	6 13-ounce cans
EGGS, hard-cooked, quartered	24
TOAST, lightly buttered	25 slices

Procedure

1. Make a cream sauce of butter, flour, cream, and seasonings. Add sherry.
2. Add fish, shrimp, tuna, and eggs.
3. Turn into baking pans or individual casseroles.
4. Cut toast in strips. Arrange on top of fish mixture. Bake in oven at 350°F. for about 30 minutes.

Note

Crabmeat or lobster may be used in place of flaked fish, shrimp or tuna, if desired.

TUNA-ITALIENNE BEAN CASSEROLE →

Yield: 24 portions

Ingredients	
TUNA, drained, flaked	3-1/4 pounds
ITALIAN GREEN BEANS, FROZEN, CUT	3-1/2 pounds
BLEU CHEESE DRESSING, CREAMY TYPE	1-1/2 cups
SOUR CREAM	3 cups
BUTTER or MARGARINE, melted	1/3 cup
BREAD CRUMBS, soft	1-1/2 quarts

CURRY SALMON BALLS

Yield: 12-1/2 pounds, 50 portions (2 balls each)

Ingredients	
WATER, boiling	2 quarts
INSTANT MASHED POTATO GRANULES	2 pounds
MILK, scalded	3 cups
EGGS, unbeaten	10 (2 cups)
LEMON JUICE	1/3 cup
SALT	1 tablespoon
PEPPER	1/2 teaspoon
CURRY POWDER	4 teaspoons
ONION, finely chopped	1/2 cup
PARSLEY, finely chopped	1/2 cup
SALMON, drained, flaked	4 pounds

Procedure

1. Pour boiling water into mixer bowl. Gradually add mashed potato granules, whipping at medium speed until well blended (about 1 minute).
2. Add milk gradually, then eggs, then lemon juice, whipping until light and fluffy. Mix in salt, pepper, curry powder, onion, parsley, and salmon.
3. Shape into balls, using No. 20 scoop. If desired, roll in flour or other coating mixture. Fry in deep fat at 375°F. for about 3 minutes, or until golden brown.
4. Serve hot with egg and parsley cream sauce.

Procedure

1. Place flaked tuna in a 2-gallon bowl.
2. Cook frozen beans in a small amount of salted water until almost done; drain.
3. Combine beans and tuna.
4. Combine cheese dressing and sour cream; mix until blended.
5. Alternate 2 layers each of tuna mixture and dressing in a greased 12-inch by 20-inch by 2-1/2-inch steam table pan. With a small spatula, make air spaces so that dressing can seep through to the bottom.
6. Combine butter with soft bread crumbs; sprinkle over top of pan.
7. Bake in oven at 350°F. for 30 minutes, or until crumbs are browned.

SALMON CROQUETTES

Yield: 150 portions

Ingredients

CELERY, chopped	3-3/4 quarts
ONION, chopped	2-1/4 quarts
SHORTENING	as needed
SALMON, drained, flaked	30 pounds
BREAD CRUMBS, soft	2-1/4 gallon
SALT	6 tablespoons
PEPPER	1 tablespoon
LEMON JUICE	1-1/2 cups
EGGS, beaten	18
MILK	3-1/4 quarts
WORCESTERSHIRE SAUCE	1/2 cup
BREAD CRUMBS, dry	1 gallon

Procedure

1. Saute celery and onion in shortening until tender but not brown.
2. Combine with salmon, soft bread crumbs, salt, pepper, lemon juice, beaten eggs, milk, and Worcestershire sauce.
3. Shape into croquettes, using a cone-shaped No. 16 scoop.
4. Coat with dry bread crumbs.
5. Fry in hot deep fat until brown.

TUNA PINWHEELS →

Yield: 48 portions

Ingredients

PEAS, FROZEN, thawed	1-3/4 quarts
WATER, boiling	as needed
TUNA, drained, flaked	3-1/4 pounds
CREAM of MUSHROOM SOUP, CONDENSED	1 51-ounce can
BISCUIT MIX	5 pounds
CREAM of MUSHROOM SOUP, CONDENSED	2 51-ounce cans
MILK	1 cup

HEARTY SALMON LOAF

Yield: 24 portions

Ingredients

SALMON, PINK, drained	8 16-ounce cans
ONION, finely chopped	1-1/2 cups (9 ounces)
CELERY, chopped	2 cups (9 ounces)
ROUND SESAME BREAD WAFERS, finely rolled	3 cups crumbs (9 ounces)
MILK	2 cups
EGGS, beaten	8
BLACK PEPPER	1/2 teaspoon
PIMIENTO PIECES	12 ounces
PARSLEY SPRIGS	as needed

Procedure

1. Break up salmon with fork. Add onion, celery, crumbs, milk, eggs, and pepper; mix well.
2. Cut 12 strips from pimiento pieces, reserve. Chop rest of pimiento, add to salmon mixture.
3. Pack into two 9-inch spring-form pan rims, placed in greased baking pans. Remove rims.
4. Bake in oven at 375°F. for 1 hour or until done.
5. Garnish with parsley and reserved pimiento strips. Cut into wedges. Serve with tomato, mushroom, or cream sauce with chopped parsley and eggs.

Procedure

1. Cover peas with boiling water; heat to boiling point; drain at once.
2. Combine 1 quart of the peas with tuna and one can of soup.
3. Prepare biscuit mix according to package directions for rolled biscuits. Divide dough into 3 parts.
4. Roll each piece of dough into a 15-inch square, 1/2 inch thick. Spread each square with about 1-1/4 quarts of tuna mixture; roll as for jelly roll.
5. Cut each roll into 16 slices, 3/4 inch thick. Place, cut side down, on greased baking sheet.
6. Bake in oven at 450°F. for 22 to 25 minutes or until done.
7. Combine the remaining 2 cans of soup with milk and remaining peas. Heat over low heat, stirring occasionally, until hot.
8. Serve rolls hot, with sauce.

TUNA CURRY

Yield: 50 portions, 2/3 cup curry, 3/4 cup rice

Ingredients

TUNA in OIL, SOLID PACK, drained	10 13-ounce cans
MUSHROOM SOUP, CONDENSED	2 50-ounce cans
OIL DRAINED FROM TUNA and LIGHT CREAM to equal	1-3/4 quarts
CURRY POWDER	1/4 cup
LIQUID HOT PEPPER SEASONING	1 tablespoon
RICE, cooked	2-1/2 gallons

Procedure

1. Drain tuna, reserving oil. Break tuna into 1-inch chunks.
2. Mix soup, oil from tuna and cream, curry powder, and hot pepper seasoning.
3. Add tuna; heat.
4. Serve with hot cooked rice. Suggested accompaniments: chutney, raisins, flaked coconut, chopped hard-cooked eggs, diced candied ginger, sliced green onions, and salted peanuts.

Note

Crabmeat, lobster, or shrimp may be used instead of tuna.

TOWN CLUB TATER AND COD

Yield: 48 portions

Ingredients

POTATOES, CHEF SPECIALS, 14- to 16-OUNCE SIZE	24
BUTTER	1/2 pound
EGG YOLKS, slightly beaten	12 (1 cup)
SALT	3 tablespoons
WHITE PEPPER, GROUND	1 teaspoon
NUTMEG, GROUND	1 teaspoon
BUTTER, melted	1/4 pound
EGGS, hard-cooked	24
CODFISH, CREAMED	1-1/2 gallons
PIMIENTO STRIPS	48

Procedure

1. Bake potatoes until tender. Cut in half lengthwise; scoop out potato, reserving shells.
2. Mash hot potatoes; beat in butter, egg yolks, and seasonings.
3. Refill potato shells with seasoned mixture, swirling top with a spatula.
4. Drizzle each portion of potato with 1/2 teaspoon melted butter. Bake in oven at 375°F. for 15 to 20 minutes or until tops of potato are lightly browned.
5. Slice eggs. Arrange overlapping slices in a row on top of each potato allowing 1/2 egg per portion.
6. Ladle 1/2 cup creamed codfish across each potato. Garnish with pimiento.

SALMON, NOODLES, AND MUSHROOMS

Yield: 50 portions, approximately 3/4 cup

Ingredients

NOODLES	1-1/2 pounds
ONION, chopped	1-1/2 cups
BUTTER or MARGARINE	1 pound
FLOUR	3/4 cup (3 ounces)
SALT	4 teaspoons
PEPPER	1/2 teaspoon
MILK	3 quarts
WORCESTERSHIRE SAUCE	2-1/2 teaspoons
PIMIENTO, drained, chopped	2 4-ounce cans
MUSHROOMS, STEMS and PIECES, drained	8 8-ounce cans
MUSHROOM LIQUID	1 quart
BUTTER or MARGARINE	1/2 pound
SALMON, flaked	9 1-pound cans
BREAD CUBES	1 quart

Procedure

1. Cook noodles in boiling salted water. Drain in colander.
2. Saute onion in first amount of butter until softened but not browned.
3. Blend in flour, salt, and pepper. Add milk. Cook until thickened, stirring with wire whip. Add Worcestershire sauce and pimiento.
4. Drain mushrooms, reserving required amount of liquid.
5. Add mushroom liquid to sauce. Lightly brown mushrooms in the remaining butter; add to cream sauce.
6. Put a layer of noodles in each of two greased 12-inch by 18-inch baking pans, then a layer of flaked salmon. Cover with sauce and sprinkle tops with bread cubes. Dribble a little butter over the cubes.
7. Bake in oven at 375°F. for about 40 minutes, until heated through and bread cubes are brown.

SPAGHETTI AND SALMON CASSEROLE →

Yield: 24 portions

Ingredients

SALT	1/2 cup
WATER, boiling	4 to 6 gallons
SPAGHETTI	4 pounds
CREAM of CELERY SOUP, CONDENSED	4 10-1/2 ounce cans (1-1/4 quarts)
EVAPORATED MILK, undiluted	4 13-ounce cans (6-2/3 cups)
SALMON, drained	4 1-pound cans
OLIVES, GREEN, PIMIENTO-STUFFED, sliced	1 cup
ONION SALT	1 teaspoon
PEPPER	1 teaspoon

TUNA RAREBIT

Yield: 50 portions

Ingredients

BUTTER or MARGARINE	12 ounces
FLOUR	5 ounces
MILK	1 gallon
CHEESE, SHARP, grated or ground	1-1/2 pounds
WORCESTERSHIRE SAUCE	1/3 cup
SALT	1 tablespoon
INSTANT GRANULATED GARLIC	1 teaspoon
EGGS, hard-cooked, chopped	9
GREEN PEPPER, chopped	1 cup
PIMIENTO, chopped	1/4 cup
TUNA, flaked	5 pounds

Procedure

1. Melt butter; blend in flour. Gradually stir in milk. Cook and stir until smooth and thickened.
2. Add cheese, Worcestershire sauce, salt, and garlic; stir until cheese is melted.
3. Add remaining ingredients; heat through.
4. Serve in individual casseroles over rice, noodles, or toast triangles.

Procedure

1. Add salt to boiling water. Add spaghetti gradually so that water continues to boil. Cook, uncovered, stirring occasionally, until tender. Drain in colander.

2. Combine soup and evaporated milk; mix well. Add remaining ingredients; mix lightly.

3. Combine spaghetti and salmon mixture. Turn into individual casseroles or a greased 12-inch by 18-inch baking pan. Bake in oven at 350°F. for 30 minutes, or until thoroughly heated.

TUNA AND NOODLES

Yield: 48 portions

Ingredients

NOODLES	3 pounds
MILK	3-1/2 quarts
ONION, finely chopped	1 cup
BUTTER or MARGARINE	14 ounces
FLOUR	7 ounces
SALT	3 tablespoons
PEPPER	1/2 teaspoon
MUSHROOMS, sliced	4 8-ounce cans
TUNA, flaked	6 13-ounce cans
BREAD CUBES, soft	1-1/2 quarts
BUTTER, melted	2 ounces

Procedure

1. Cook noodles in boiling salted water; drain.

2. Combine milk and chopped onion; heat.

3. Blend first amount of butter and flour. Gradually add hot milk mixture; cook and stir until thickened. Add salt and pepper. Add mushrooms.

4. Spread a layer of noodles in greased baking pans; cover with a layer of tuna. Top with sauce. Sprinkle with cubed bread; drizzle with melted butter.

5. Bake in oven at 350°F. for 30 to 40 minutes or until heated through and top is browned.

SALMON-SEAFOOD LOAF

Yield: 6 9-inch by 5-inch by 3-inch loaves or 2 12-inch by 20-inch by 2-inch pans, 48 portions

Ingredients

FISH, cooked flaked	1 gallon
SALMON, PINK, flaked	2 quarts
CELERY, chopped (including tops)	1 quart
WHITE SAUCE (VERY THICK)	1 quart
TOMATO SAUCE	2 cups
BREAD CRUMBS, dry	2 cups
LEMON JUICE	2 tablespoons
EGGS, beaten	6

Procedure

1. Combine ingredients thoroughly.
2. Turn into six 9-inch by 5-inch by 3-inch loaf pans. Bake in oven at 350°F. for 1 hour.

SAUCES FOR SALMON-SEAFOOD LOAF

Yield: about 1 gallon

Ingredients

No. 1	
TOMATO SAUCE	1 quart
CREAM of MUSHROOM SOUP	3 quarts
No. 2	
TOMATO SAUCE	1 No. 10 can
BROWN SUGAR, packed measure	1/2 cup
PARSLEY, chopped	1/4 cup
No. 3	
WHITE SAUCE, MEDIUM	3 quarts
PIMIENTO, chopped	1 cup
GREEN PEPPER, slivered	1 cup
MUSHROOMS, STEMS and PIECES, drained	1 cup
No. 4	
WHITE SAUCE, MEDIUM	3 quarts
OLIVES, RIPE, chopped	2 cups

Procedure

Combine ingredients; heat for service.

Tunaburger-Cheesewich

Kellogg Company

INDIVIDUAL CHEESE-FISH POTPIES

Yield: 24 portions

Ingredients	
MARGARINE	3/4 cup (6 ounces)
FLOUR	3/4 cup (3 ounces)
MILK	1-1/2 quarts
CHEESE, PROCESS AMERICAN, shredded	1-1/2 pounds
FISH, cooked, boned, flaked	3 pounds
POTATOES, cooked, diced	1-1/2 quarts
CELERY, diced, cooked	3/4 quart
GREEN PEPPER, chopped, cooked	1-1/2 cups
PIMIENTO, chopped	3/4 cup
SALT	3 tablespoons
PEPPER	1-1/4 teaspoons
*POTPIE TOPS, baked	24

*Rounds cut from pie pastry to fit casserole tops.

Procedure

1. Make a cream sauce with the margarine, flour, and milk. When thickened and smooth, add cheese; stir until melted.

2. Combine the cheese sauce, fish, vegetables, and seasonings. Mix lightly. Keep hot.

3. For each pie, portion 1 cup of the hot cheese and fish mixture into an individual casserole; cover with a baked potpie top. Serve hot.

FISH AND CHEESE CASSEROLE

Yield: 24 portions

Ingredients

MILK	1-1/2 quarts
BUTTER or MARGARINE	1/4 pound
BREAD CRUMBS, soft	1 quart
PIMIENTO, chopped	1/2 cup
PARSLEY, chopped	1/2 cup
ONION, minced	1/2 cup
CHEESE, AMERICAN CHEDDAR, grated	1-1/2 pounds
SALT	2 teaspoons
PEPPER	1/2 teaspoon
PAPRIKA	dash
EGGS, well beaten	12
FISH or SEAFOOD, CANNED or cooked	2 quarts

Procedure

1. Heat milk with butter; pour over bread crumbs in mixing bowl.
2. Add pimiento, parsley, onion, cheese, and seasonings. Mix well.
3. Slowly stir in eggs.
4. Arrange fish in 2 oiled 10-inch by 12-inch steam table pans; pour the cheese mixture over the fish.
5. Set the pans in a larger pan. Make a water bath, adding hot water to within 1 inch from rim.
6. Bake in oven at 325°F. for 1 hour and 15 minutes, or until silver knife inserted in center comes out clean.

PIMIENTO TUNA DIVAN

Yield: 50 portions

Ingredients

BROCCOLI SPEARS, FROZEN	5 pounds
CREAM of MUSHROOM SOUP, CONDENSED	2 50-ounce cans
EVAPORATED MILK	2-1/2 cups
TUNA, flaked	5 pounds
PIMIENTO STRIPS	1 15-ounce can
PIMIENTO BISCUITS, hot	50

Procedure

1. Cook broccoli until just tender; drain. Keep hot.
2. Combine soup and milk (use reconstituted milk, if desired).
3. Add tuna and pimiento to sauce. Check flavor and add seasoning, if desired.
4. To serve: split biscuit; place a few pieces of broccoli across bottom half. Ladle 4 ounces of tuna mixture over the broccoli, reserving a small amount in the ladle. Top with remaining half biscuit, and the reserved tuna mixture. Garnish with parsley or a piece of lettuce and a few pickle slices, if desired.

TUNA, CANTON STYLE

Yield: 48 2/3-cup portions

Ingredients

ONION, chopped	1-1/2 cups
CELERY, sliced	2 pounds
BUTTER or MARGARINE	1-1/2 pounds
PIMIENTO, chopped	9 ounces
SWEET PICKLE RELISH	1 pound
CREAM of MUSHROOM SOUP, CONDENSED	3 51-ounce cans
TUNA, drained, flaked	4-1/2 pounds
PIMIENTO STRIPS	48

Procedure

1. Saute onion and celery in butter until tender-crisp. Add pimiento, relish, soup, and tuna; heat.
2. Serve over fried noodles or fluffy rice. Garnish with pimiento strip.

TUNA PIE WITH CHEESE BISCUITS* ⟶

Yield: 30 portions

Ingredients	
MARGARINE	10 ounces
FLOUR	5 ounces (1-1/4 cups)
SALT	1-1/2 teaspoons
PEPPER	1/2 teaspoon
MILK	2-1/2 quarts
GREEN PEPPER, diced	1/2 pound
ONION, diced	4 ounces
MARGARINE	2 ounces
TUNA, drained, flaked	7 7-ounce cans
LEMON JUICE	1/4 cup
CHEESE BISCUITS	30

*CHEESE BISCUITS

Yield: 30 biscuits, 1-1/2 ounces each

Ingredients	
FLOUR	1-1/4 pounds
BAKING POWDER	2 tablespoons
SALT	2 teaspoons
SHORTENING	6-1/2 ounces
CHEESE, CHEDDAR, grated	5 ounces
MILK	1-3/4 cups

Procedure

1. Combine flour, baking powder, and salt, mixing thoroughly.
2. Cut in shortening with pastry blender until mixture resembles coarse meal. Add cheese.
3. Add milk; mix until soft dough is formed.
4. Turn out on a lightly floured board; knead 30 seconds. Roll 1/2 inch thick; cut with floured 2-1/2-inch cutter.

Procedure

1. Melt first amount of margarine; blend in flour, salt, and pepper. Add milk gradually; cook and stir until thickened and smooth.
2. Saute green pepper and onion in remaining margarine until softened but not brown.
3. Add sauteed vegetables and tuna to sauce; stir in lemon juice.
4. Ladle into individual casseroles; top each with a cheese biscuit.
5. Bake in oven at 450°F. for 30 minutes or until biscuit is done.

MUSHROOM SALMON LOAF

Yield: 48 portions

Ingredients

SALMON	8 1-pound cans
CARROTS, grated	2 quarts (2 pounds)
CELERY, finely chopped	1 quart
ONION, finely chopped	2 cups
BREAD CRUMBS, finely sifted	1 quart (1 pound)
CREAM of MUSHROOM SOUP, undiluted	1 51-ounce can
EGGS, slightly beaten	8
LEMON JUICE	1/2 cup

Procedure

1. Combine salmon, carrots, celery, onion, and bread crumbs; toss to mix.
2. Mix soup with eggs; add lemon juice. Combine with salmon mixture.
3. Turn into 6 greased loaf pans 8-1/2 inch by 4-1/4 inch by 2-1/2 inch lined with waxed paper, using 2-1/2 pounds salmon mixture per loaf.
4. Set pans in hot water; bake in oven at 325°F. for 1-1/2 hours. Slice and serve with mushroom sauce.

CHOPSTICK TUNA

Yield: 25 portions

Ingredients	
ONION, sliced	2-1/4 pounds
CELERY, sliced	2-1/4 pounds
MUSHROOMS, sliced	1/2 pound
SHORTENING	1/4 pound
CREAM of MUSHROOM SOUP, CONDENSED	1 quart
BAMBOO SHOOTS, sliced	1-1/2 cups
WATER CHESTNUTS, sliced	1-1/4 cups
TUNA, flaked	2-1/2 pounds
SOY SAUCE	2 tablespoons
SALT	1 tablespoon
RICE, cooked	4-1/2 quarts
FRIED CHINESE NOODLES	1-1/2 pounds
MANDARIN ORANGE SECTIONS, drained	1 quart

Procedure

1. Saute onion, celery, and mushrooms in shortening until onions look "wilted" and glossy. Add mushroom soup; simmer 10 minutes.
2. Add bamboo shoots, chestnuts, tuna, soy sauce, and salt. Heat to blend thoroughly. (Use a fork for stirring to avoid breaking up mixture.)
3. Serve over hot rice. Sprinkle top with fried noodles. Garnish with mandarin orange sections.

Flavored Fruit Accompaniment for Cooked Fish

Wheat Flour Institute

Fish Portion Entrees

SEA BOUNTY IMPERIAL

Yield: 24 portions

Ingredients

SOY SAUCE	3/4 cup
SUGAR	1 tablespoon
GINGER, GROUND	1 tablespoon
MUSHROOMS, FRESH, sliced	2 pounds
SCALLIONS, sliced	3 cups
PEANUT OIL	1/2 cup
GREEN PEPPERS, coarsely chopped	4
PIMIENTO, cut	1 cup
BAMBOO SHOOTS, diced	2 cups
WATER CHESTNUTS, sliced	2 cups
CUCUMBER, peeled, diced	2 cups
CHICKEN BROTH	1 quart
SPINACH LEAVES, torn into pieces	2 pounds
CORNSTARCH	1/4 cup
WATER	1/2 cup
FISH PORTIONS, BREADED, SHAPED, 4-OUNCE	24
RICE, cooked, hot	4-3/4 quarts

Procedure

1. Combine soy sauce, sugar, and ginger.
2. Saute mushrooms and scallions in oil until wilted. Add green peppers, pimiento, bamboo shoots, water chestnuts, cucumber, chicken broth, and soy sauce mixture. Cover; simmer 10 minutes, until vegetables are tender but still crisp.
3. Add spinach; stir.
4. Blend cornstarch with water; slowly stir into vegetable mixture. Cook until mixture bubbles and is slightly thickened.
5. Fry fish portions in deep fat at 360° to 400°F. about 3 minutes. Drain on absorbent paper.
6. For each portion, allow 3/4 cup rice, 3/4 cup vegetable mixture, and one 4-ounce fish portion. To serve Chinese-restaurant style, arrange 2 fish portions on rice; surround with vegetable mixture.

FISH STICKS WITH TOMATO-ZUCCHINI SAUCE

Yield: 24 portions

Ingredients

FISH STICKS, FROZEN, PRECOOKED, 2-ounce size	48
OLIVE OIL	1 cup
GARLIC, chopped	3 cloves
ONION, chopped	3 cups
FLOUR	3 ounces
TOMATOES AND ZUCCHINI	1 No. 10 can
SHELL MACARONI, cooked	1-1/2 gallons

Procedure

1. Heat fish sticks in oven at 400°F. for 10 to 12 minutes; keep warm.
2. Heat olive oil; add garlic and onion; saute until golden. Blend in flour. Slowly add tomatoes and zucchini; cook and stir until thickened.
3. To serve, put macaroni in serving dishes allowing 1 cup per portion. Arrange fish sticks on macaroni; top each portion with 1/2 cup sauce.

HUSH PUPPIES

Yield: approximately 96, 1 ounce each

Ingredients

CORN MEAL, COARSE	4-1/4 pounds
BAKING POWDER	1 ounce
SALT	1-1/2 tablespoons
MILK, WHOLE	3 pounds, 2 ounces
WATER	1 pound
EGGS	4
ONION, finely chopped	3/4 to 1 cup

Procedure

1. Mix together corn meal, baking powder, and salt. Add milk and water; mix.
2. Blend in eggs and onion.
3. Form dough into small (1-ounce) cakes.
4. Fry in deep fat at 375°F. until browned. Drain well. Serve hot with fried fish, breaded fish portions, or fish sticks.

BREADED FISH FILLET, ONION-CHEESE SAUCE →

Yield: 24 portions

Ingredients

FISH PORTIONS, FILLET-SHAPED, FROZEN, BREADED	24
ONIONS, FROZEN, CREAMED	36 ounces
MILK	2 cups
CHEESE SAUCE	4-1/2 cups
BROCCOLI, FROZEN, CHOPPED, cooked, drained	7 pounds
PIMIENTO, STRIPS	24

FRIED FISH, CHICAGO CHINATOWN

Yield: 24 portions

Ingredients

SHORTENING	4 ounces
BEAN SPROUTS, FRESH	6 pounds
SALT	2-1/2 tablespoons
SUGAR	1 tablespoon
MONOSODIUM GLUTAMATE	1-1/2 teaspoons
SOY SAUCE	1-1/2 cups
CHICKEN BROTH or VEGETABLE BROTH or WATER	1-1/2 cups
FISH PORTIONS, FROZEN, BREADED	24
MAYONNAISE or SALAD DRESSING	1 quart
SOY SAUCE	1/4 cup

Procedure

1. Melt shortening in heavy pan or steam-jacketed kettle. Add bean sprouts, salt sugar, and monosodium glutamate. Cook, stirring constantly, for 3 to 4 minutes. Handle carefully to avoid breaking sprouts.
2. Combine first amount of soy sauce and broth; pour over sprouts. Continue cooking and stirring for 5 minutes, making sure that the hot liquid reaches all the sprouts. Turn into steam table pan.
3. Fry fish portions. Arrange on top of sprouts.
4. Mix mayonnaise and remaining soy sauce. Serve with fish.

Procedure

1. Fry fillets in deep fat at 360° to 375°F. for 3 minutes. Drain. Keep warm.

2. Combine onions, milk, and cheese sauce; stir over low heat until sauce is smooth.

3. To serve, put broccoli in serving dishes, allowing 3/4 cup per portion. Arrange fillets on broccoli; top each portion with 1/3 cup onion sauce. Garnish with pimiento strips.

WAKE-UP FISH A L'ORANGE

Yield: 25 portions

Ingredients

WATER, boiling	1 quart
SUGAR	12 ounces
CORNSTARCH	1-1/4 ounces
ORANGE JUICE	2 cups
ORANGE RIND, grated	1 tablespoon
LEMON JUICE	2 tablespoons
BUTTER	2 ounces
SALT	1/2 teaspoon
FISH PORTIONS, BREADED,* 3-OUNCE	4-3/4 pounds

Procedure

1. Bring water to boil.

2. Mix sugar and cornstarch; add to boiling water, stirring until mixture begins to thicken. Cook until clear and thickened.

3. Remove from heat; blend in orange juice, orange rind, lemon juice, butter, and salt.

4. Hold sauce over hot water until serving time. Add orange juice, if necessary, to thin to desired consistency.

5. Fry in deep fat or oven-finish breaded fish portions according to package directions. Serve portion topped with 2 ounces of orange sauce.

*Use raw for deep frying; precooked for oven-finishing.

BAKED FISH PORTIONS WITH TOMATO SAUCE

Yield: 25 portions

Ingredients

FISH PORTIONS, FROZEN, RAW, UNBREADED, 4-OUNCE	25
ONION, chopped	1 cup
GREEN PEPPER, chopped	1/4 cup
SHORTENING or COOKING OIL	1/3 cup
FLOUR	1/2 cup
TOMATOES, CANNED	1 quart
SALT	1-1/2 tablespoons
CLOVES, GROUND	dash
BAY LEAVES, crushed	dash
SUGAR	2 teaspoons
BLACK PEPPER	1/2 teaspoon

Procedure

1. Place frozen fish portions in a single layer in well-greased baking pans.
2. Saute onion and green pepper in shortening or oil until tender. Blend in flour.
3. Add tomatoes and seasonings. Cook and stir until thickened.
4. Cover fish with sauce. Bake in oven at 350°F. for 30 to 40 minutes or until fish flakes easily when tested with a fork.
5. Serve on a bed of buttered shell macaroni, if desired.

FISKE MED DILLSAS

Yield: 16 or 32 portions

Ingredients

FISH FILLETS or FISH PORTIONS, FROZEN, BREADED	16 or 32
BUTTERMILK	2 cups
SOUR CREAM	1 quart
ONION, thinly sliced	1/2 cup
SALT	1 teaspoon
DILL WEED, DRIED	1 tablespoon

Procedure

1. Prepare fish portions or fillets according to label directions.
2. Blend buttermilk and sour cream. Add onion, salt, and dill weed; mix.
3. Serve one or two pieces of fish. Ladle approximately 3 ounces of sauce over fish.

WIKIWIKI L'A

(See picture, page 72)

Yield: 16 or 32 portions

Ingredients

FISH FILLETS or FISH PORTIONS, FROZEN, BREADED	16 or 32
SWEET and SOUR SAUCE	1 No. 5 can

Procedure

1. Prepare fish portions or fillets according to label directions.
2. Heat sauce.
3. Serve one or two pieces of fish. Ladle approximately 3 ounces of sauce over fish.

Fish Entrees

Fish Fillets a la King

Bureau of Commercial Fisheries, USDA

LOBSTER-STUFFED FILLETS

Yield: 25 portions

Ingredients

ONION, finely chopped	2 ounces
SHALLOTS, minced	2 ounces
BUTTER or MARGARINE	12 ounces
PAPRIKA	2 teaspoons
MONOSODIUM GLUTAMATE	2 teaspoons
BREAD CRUMBS, fine, dry	12 ounces
LOBSTER MEAT, finely chopped	12 ounces
SHERRY	2 ounces (1/4 cup)
NEWBURG SAUCE, cooled	1-1/4 cups
FISH FILLETS, SKINLESS, cut into thin 4-inch pieces	8 pounds
SALT	as needed
PEPPER	as needed
BUTTER or MARGARINE, melted	8 ounces
NEWBURG SAUCE, hot	2-1/2 quarts
WATERCRESS	as needed

Procedure

1. Saute onion and shallots in first amount of butter until tender but not brown. Blend in paprika and monosodium glutamate.
2. Remove from heat. Add bread crumbs, lobster, sherry, and cooled Newburg Sauce; mix.
3. Place mound of stuffing on each piece of fish. Roll; fasten with wooden picks.
4. Place in well-greased baking pans. Sprinkle with salt and pepper. Brush with melted butter.
5. Bake in oven at 375°F. for 30 minutes or until done.
6. To serve, remove picks; place fillets in individual casseroles. Add about 3 ounces hot Newburg Sauce to each portion. Glaze quickly under broiler.
7. Garnish with watercress.

BROILED FISH AMANDINE →

Yield: 24 portions

Ingredients	
FISH FILLETS or STEAKS	8 pounds
COOKING OIL	3/4 cup
SALT	as needed
PAPRIKA	as needed
BUTTER	1/2 pound
ALMONDS, BLANCHED, SLIVERED	1-1/2 cups
LEMON JUICE	1/2 cup
LIQUID HOT PEPPER SEASONING	1/2 teaspoon
PARSLEY, chopped	1/2 cup

HERB-BROILED FISH

Yield: 50 portions

Ingredients	
BLUEFISH or MACKEREL FILLETS, 4- to 5-OUNCE	16 pounds
SALT	3 tablespoons
PEPPERCORNS, WHOLE	2 tablespoons
OIL	2 cups
CIDER VINEGAR	2 cups
WATER	2 cups
LEMON JUICE	1 cup
GARLIC SALT	1 teaspoon
INSTANT MINCED ONION	1/2 cup
PARSLEY FLAKES	1/4 cup
BAY LEAVES	3
FENNEL SEED	1 teaspoon
WHITE WINE (optional)	1 cup

Procedure

1. Place fish fillets in a flat pan.
2. Combine remaining ingredients; mix well. Pour over fish; refrigerate for three hours, turning occasionally, in marinade.
3. When ready to serve, drain well; broil. Or, if desired, coat lightly with flour and panfry. Serve with drawn butter and a lemon wedge.

Procedure

1. Divide fillets into portions.
2. Dip fillets or steaks in oil; place in well-greased shallow pan or on heavy foil. Sprinkle with salt and paprika.
3. Broil, without turning, until fish flakes easily with a fork.
4. Melt butter over low heat. Add almonds; saute, stirring, until golden. Add lemon juice and hot pepper seasoning.
5. Serve almond sauce over fish; sprinkle with parsley.

SAVORY BAKED FISH

Yield: 100 portions

Ingredients

FISH FILLETS, PORTION-CUT, SQUARE, ice-glazed	100
TOMATO, sliced	100 slices (approx. 20 medium tomatoes)
ONION, sliced	100 slices (approx. 20 medium onions)
BUTTER or MARGARINE, melted	2 pounds
LEMON JUICE	2 cups
SALT	5 tablespoons
PEPPER	1 tablespoon
BAY LEAVES, SMALL	100

Procedure

1. Thaw fish fillets. Place in greased shallow baking pans.
2. Arrange a tomato slice on each fillet. Top with an onion slice.
3. Combine melted butter, lemon juice, salt, and pepper. Pour over fish in pans.
4. Place a bay leaf on each portion.
5. Cover pans with inverted baking pans of the same size or with aluminum foil. Bake in oven at 375°F. for 30 minutes or until done.

TASTY FISH FRY
(Dip for Breading)

Yield: 4-3/4 cups

Ingredients

TOMATO SAUCE	1 quart
WORCESTERSHIRE SAUCE	1/2 cup
LEMON JUICE	1/4 cup
POULTRY SEASONING	1/4 teaspoon

Procedure

1. Combine ingredients. Let stand for several minutes to blend flavors.

2. To use as a dip for breading: Clean fish, wipe dry. Roll fish lightly in flour, dip in sauce. Coat with a mixture of cracker crumbs and flour. Fry in deep fat at 375° to 385°F.

FISH FILLET ESPAGNA

Yield: 1 portion

Ingredients

FISH FILLET, FRESH or FROZEN	8 ounces
OLIVE OIL	1 tablespoon
ONION, chopped	1 tablespoon
GREEN PEPPER, chopped	1 tablespoon
PIMIENTO, diced	1 tablespoon
GARLIC POWDER	dash
SALT	as needed
PEPPER	as needed
CHICKEN BROTH	3 to 4 tablespoons

Procedure

1. Thaw frozen fish.
2. Saute fillet in olive oil, turning once. Remove to baking dish.
3. Add onion, pepper, pimiento, and garlic powder to same pan; saute lightly. Spread over fish. Sprinkle with salt and pepper. Add broth.
4. Bake in oven at 350°F. until fish flakes when tested with a fork. Serve with saffron rice and avocado slices, if desired.

FRIED FISH WITH DYNASTY SAUCE

Yield: 24 portions

Ingredients

FISH FILLETS	8 pounds
ONION, finely chopped	1 cup
GINGER ROOT, FRESH, chopped	2 tablespoons
SOY SAUCE	2 tablespoons
SALT	2 tablespoons
SHERRY	2 tablespoons
PEPPER	3/4 teaspoon
CORNSTARCH	as needed
COOKING OIL	as needed
SUGAR	1-1/2 cups
CORNSTARCH	1/3 cup
CIDER VINEGAR	4-1/2 cups
GREEN ONIONS, chopped	1-1/2 cups
RED PEPPERS, cut julienne	3 cups
CARROTS, cut julienne	3 cups
SWEET GHERKINS, sliced	1 quart
GINGER ROOT, FRESH, chopped	3 tablespoons

Procedure

1. Cut fish fillets into 5-ounce portions.
2. Combine onion, first amount of ginger root, soy sauce, salt, sherry, and pepper. Rub mixture into fish; let stand for 1/2 hour.
3. Roll fish in cornstarch; let stand for 5 minutes.
4. Fry fish in hot oil at 350°F. for 10 minutes or until lightly browned. Drain. Keep warm.
5. Mix sugar and measured amount of cornstarch; add vinegar. Heat mixture; add green onions, red peppers, carrots, pickles, and remaining ginger root. Cook over low heat, stirring constantly, until thickened.
6. Serve sauce over fish.

FILLETS IN FRESNO RAISIN CREAM SAUCE ➔

Yield: 24 portions

Ingredients

FISH FILLETS	24 portions
CREAM, HEAVY	1 quart
ONION, grated	1/4 cup
LEMON RIND, grated	1 tablespoon
LEMON JUICE, freshly squeezed	6 tablespoons
RAISINS, GOLDEN	2 cups
SALT	as needed
WHITE PEPPER	as needed
LEMON SLICES	as needed

BAKED FISH IN LEMON HORSERADISH SAUCE

Yield: 48 portions

Ingredients

FISH FILLETS, FROZEN or FRESH	12 pounds
BUTTER or MARGARINE	1 pound
ONION, chopped	3/4 cup
FLOUR	1/2 cup
SALT	2 teaspoons
WATER	1 quart
LEMON JUICE, fresh	1/2 cup
PIMIENTO, chopped	1/2 cup
CAPERS	1/2 cup
HORSERADISH	1/4 cup

Procedure

1. Divide fillets into 48 4-ounce portions; place in shallow baking pans.
2. Melt butter. Add onion; saute until tender.
3. Blend in flour and salt. Add water gradually, stirring constantly. Bring to a boil; cook 4 minutes.
4. Add remaining ingredients; pour over fish.
5. Bake in oven at 375°F. for about 35 minutes or until fish flakes easily when tested with a fork.

Procedure

1. Arrange fillets in baking pan.
2. Combine cream, onion, lemon rind, lemon juice, and raisins. Season with salt and pepper. Pour over fish.
3. Bake in oven at 400°F. until fish flakes when tested with a fork.
4. Spoon sauce over each portion. Garnish with lemon slices.

POACHED FISH FILLETS ON VEGETABLES PAYSANNE

Yield: 2 portions

Ingredients

CARROTS, coarsely grated	1-1/2 cups
ONION, finely chopped	1/2 cup
CELERY, finely chopped	1/2 cup
BUTTER	1/4 cup
SALT	1/2 teaspoon
SUGAR	1 teaspoon
TOMATOES, CANNED	2 cups
FISH FILLETS, FRESH or FROZEN	3 (approx. 1 pound)

Procedure

1. Saute carrots, onion, and celery lightly in butter; add salt and sugar.
2. Break up tomatoes slightly; drain. Add to vegetable mixture. Simmer a few minutes to blend flavors.
3. Poach fillets in court bouillon or stock.
4. Place a layer of vegetables in serving platter. Arrange fillets on top of vegetables. Garnish with lemon and parsley.

SHRIMP-STUFFED FISH FILLETS

Yield: 21 portions (2 rolls each)

Ingredients

ONION, finely chopped	1-1/2 ounces
SHALLOTS, minced	1-1/2 ounces
MUSHROOMS, chopped	1-1/2 ounces
BUTTER or MARGARINE, melted	8 ounces
PAPRIKA	1-1/2 teaspoons
MONOSODIUM GLUTAMATE	1-1/2 teaspoons
BREAD CRUMBS, fine, dry	10 ounces
SHRIMP, cooked, finely chopped	1 pound
CHABLIS WINE or LEMON JUICE	3 tablespoons
NEWBURG SAUCE, cooled	1 cup
SALT	as needed
FISH FILLETS, skinned, thin, 4-inch pieces	42 (7 to 8 pounds
BUTTER or MARGARINE, melted	as needed
SALT	as needed
PEPPER	as needed
NEWBURG SAUCE, hot	2 quarts

Procedure

1. Saute onion, shallots, and mushrooms in butter until tender, but not brown. Blend in paprika and monosodium glutamate.
2. Remove from heat. Add crumbs, shrimp, wine, and cooled Newburg Sauce. Season with salt.
3. Place mound of stuffing on each strip of fish; roll and fasten with wooden picks. Place in well-greased baking pans.
4. Brush with melted butter; sprinkle with salt and pepper.
5. Bake in oven at 375°F. for 30 minutes or until done.
6. Spoon hot Newburg Sauce over fish. Garnish with watercress, if desired.

BAKED FROZEN FISH FILLETS

Yield: 100 portions

Ingredients

COD or HADDOCK FILLETS, FROZEN	25 pounds
SALT	1/3 cup
PAPRIKA	1/4 cup
ONION, chopped	2-1/2 cups
GREEN PEPPER, chopped	3/4 cup
TOMATO SAUCE	2 quarts
SHORTENING, melted	2-1/4 cups
LEMON JUICE	1-1/2 cups
PARSLEY, chopped	3/4 cup

Procedure

1. Place frozen fish fillets on greased baking sheets. Sprinkle with salt and paprika.
2. Combine onion, green pepper, and tomato sauce.
3. Combine melted shortening and lemon juice. Stir into tomato mixture. Spread sauce over fish.
4. Bake in oven at 400°F. for 25 minutes or until fish flakes when tested with a fork. Serve garnished with parsley.

FISH FILLETS AMANDINE

Yield: 25 5-ounce portions

Ingredients

FISH FILLETS, FRESH or FROZEN	8 to 9 pounds
BUTTER or MARGARINE	12 ounces
ALMONDS, toasted, coarsely chopped	1 cup
LEMON JUICE	2 tablespoons
LEMON RIND, grated	3 tablespoons
SALT	1 tablespoon
PEPPER	3/4 teaspoon

Procedure

1. Arrange fillets in approximately 5-ounce portions on sheetpans.
2. Soften butter or margarine, add chopped almonds and remaining ingredients. Spread on fillets.
3. Bake in oven at 375°F. for 10 to 12 minutes.

FILLET AND RICE, LOUISIANA

Yield: 1 portion

Ingredients

ONION, minced	1 teaspoon
CELERY, minced	1 tablespoon
BUTTER or MARGARINE	2 tablespoons
RICE, cooked	1/2 cup
CHILI SAUCE	2 tablespoons
CREAM, LIGHT	3 tablespoons
SALT	1/4 teaspoon
PEPPER	dash
CAYENNE PEPPER	dash
POLLACK or OTHER FISH FILLET, FRESH or FROZEN, thawed	8 ounces
BUTTER or MARGARINE	2 tablespoons
PEAS, cooked	1/4 cup
PARSLEY or CRESS	as needed
LEMON WEDGES	2

Procedure

1. Saute onion and celery in first amount of butter until tender. Add rice, chili sauce, cream, and seasonings. Cook over low heat 4 to 5 minutes.

2. Saute fillet in remaining butter, turning once.

3. Turn hot rice mixture into an oval individual casserole or serving dish; top with fillet. Garnish with peas at one end of the dish, parsley or cress at other. Arrange lemon wedges on fish.

DEVILED FISH FILLETS

Yield: 50 portions

Ingredients

EGGS, beaten	6
LEMON JUICE	1/2 cup
WHITE SAUCE, THICK, seasoned, hot	2 quarts
CAYENNE PEPPER	1/4 teaspoon
WORCESTERSHIRE SAUCE	3 tablespoons
CELERY, minced	1/2 cup
PARSLEY, minced	1 cup
ONION, minced	1 cup
BREAD CRUMBS, WHITE, soft	1-1/4 quarts
BUTTER or MARGARINE, melted	4 ounces
BREAD CRUMBS, fine, dry	2 cups
POLLACK or OTHER FISH FILLETS, FRESH or FROZEN, thawed	50 8-ounce pieces
COOKING OIL	as needed
SALT	as needed
PEPPER	as needed

Procedure

1. Combine eggs and lemon juice.
2. Add a small amount of the hot thick sauce; blend. Stir egg mixture into hot sauce.
3. Add cayenne pepper, Worcestershire sauce, and minced vegetables. Cook and stir over low heat until very thick.
4. Add soft crumbs. Check seasoning, adding salt if necessary. Cool.
5. Combine melted butter and dry crumbs; toss to mix.
6. Arrange fillets in oiled shallow pans, placing close together but not overlapping. Brush with oil. Sprinkle with salt and pepper.
7. Using a 2-ounce scoop, drop a mound of seasoned sauce mixture on each fillet; flatten and spread to cover surface.
8. Sprinkle lightly with buttered crumbs.
9. Bake in oven at 350°F. for 30 minutes or until fish flakes with a fork.
10. Run under broiler to crisp and brown top.

BREADED FILLET, SWISS STYLE →

Yield: 1 portion

Ingredients

FISH FILLET, breaded	8 ounces
TOMATO SLICES, thin	3
CHEESE, SWISS, NATURAL	1 ounce slice
PARSLEY, chopped	as needed
PAPRIKA	dash

PLANKED FISH FILLET

Yield: 2 portions

Ingredients

FISH FILLET (SOLE, FLOUNDER, WHITEFISH, LAKE TROUT or HADDOCK)	1 10- to 12-ounce
BUTTER or MARGARINE, melted	1 tablespoon
SALT	as needed
PEPPER	as needed
SEASONED DUCHESS POTATOES	1 cup
TOMATO HALVES, broiled	2
MUSHROOM CAPS, broiled	4

Procedure

1. If fish is frozen, let thaw in refrigerator or at room temperature.
2. Brush seasoned plank lightly with melted butter. Arrange fillet on plank; brush with remaining butter. Sprinkle with salt and pepper.
3. Bake in oven at 350°F. for 20 to 25 minutes, or just until fish flakes easily when tested with a fork.
4. Pipe a border of hot Duchess Potatoes along sides of fish. Run under broiler until potatoes are delicately browned.
5. Arrange tomatoes and mushroom caps on plank. Garnish with lemon and cress, if desired.

Procedure

1. Saute fillet, or cook in deep fat.
2. Top fillet with tomato slices, then with cheese. Broil until cheese melts.
3. Sprinkle with parsley and paprika. Serve with asparagus tips and browned whole potatoes, if desired.

BOSTON BLUEFISH CHEESE CASSEROLE

Yield: 24 portions

Ingredients

BOSTON BLUEFISH, POLLACK or OTHER FISH FILLETS	5 pounds
NOODLES, dry	1 pound
WHITE SAUCE, MEDIUM	3 quarts
PAPRIKA	1 teaspoon
CHEESE, grated	8 ounces
WORCESTERSHIRE SAUCE	1-1/2 tablespoons
LEMON JUICE	1/4 cup
CHEESE, grated	8 ounces
BREAD CRUMBS, soft	2 quarts

Procedure

1. Thaw fish. Poach in salted water 15 minutes. Drain and flake.
2. Cook noodles until tender; drain.
3. Combine white sauce, paprika, first amount of cheese, Worcestershire sauce, and lemon juice. Heat and stir until cheese melts.
4. Combine sauce, flaked fish, and noodles. Pour into a 12-inch by 20-inch by 2-1/2-inch pan.
5. Combine remaining cheese and crumbs; sprinkle over top.
6. Bake in oven at 325°F. for 1 hour.

BAKED FILLETS WITH STUFFING

Yield: 25 portions

Ingredients

BACON, sliced	1 pound
BREAD, day-old	2-1/2 pounds
ONION, minced	8 ounces
CELERY, minced	8 ounces
BUTTER or MARGARINE	8 ounces
SALT	2 teaspoons
PEPPER	1 teaspoon
POULTRY SEASONING	1 tablespoon
BROTH or STOCK	1 quart
BOSTON BLUEFISH, POLLACK or OTHER FISH FILLETS, FRESH or FROZEN, thawed	25 8-ounce pieces
BUTTER, melted	8 ounces
OLIVES, STUFFED, sliced	8 ounces

Procedure

1. Cook bacon until crisp; drain; crumble.
2. Chop bread or cut into small cubes (bread should be dry).
3. Saute onion and celery in butter until tender but not brown. Combine with bread. Add seasoning; toss to mix.
4. Add broth, about one-fourth at a time; mix well. (Stuffing should be moist but not soggy.
5. Spread stuffing in a thin layer in greased shallow baking pans.
6. Arrange fillets on top of stuffing.
7. Mix melted butter, crumbled bacon, and olives; sprinkle over fillets. Bake in oven at 350°F. for 35 to 40 minutes or until fish flakes easily when tested with a fork.

BAKED HADDOCK IN NEWBURG SAUCE

Yield: 36 portions

Ingredients	
MILK	3 quarts
MARGARINE	8 ounces
SALT	2-1/2 teaspoons
WHITE PEPPER	1/2 teaspoon
PAPRIKA	1/4 teaspoon
EGG YOLKS	4
EVAPORATED MILK, undiluted	1 14-ounce can
FLOUR	8 ounces
PIMIENTO, diced	3/4 cup
SHERRY, MEDIUM DRY	1/2 cup
HADDOCK, 5-OUNCE PIECES*	36
SALT	4 teaspoons
CHEESE, SHARP, shredded	2 pounds, 4 ounces

*Frozen, pre-portioned

Procedure

1. Combine milk, margarine, salt, pepper, and paprika; heat to boiling.
2. Beat egg yolks until smooth; blend in a little of the hot mixture. Add gradually, while stirring, to remainder of hot milk mixture.
3. Blend evaporated milk with flour. Add to hot mixture; cook and stir until smooth and thickened.
4. Remove from heat. Add pimiento and sherry.
5. Divide sauce evenly into four 13-inch by 9-inch by 2-inch pans. Arrange 9 portions of fish in each pan.
6. Sprinkle 1 teaspoon of salt over fish in each pan. Top each piece of fish with 1 ounce of shredded cheese.
7. Bake in oven at 350°F. for 30 minutes.

CHILLED HADDOCK, FRESH LEMON-DILL SAUCE ➔

Yield: 30 portions, 4-1/2 cups sauce

Ingredients

HADDOCK FILLETS	30 portions
SALT	as needed
LEMON JUICE, fresh	as needed
WATER	as needed
MAYONNAISE	1 quart
WHITE WINE	3 tablespoons
LEMON RIND, grated	1 tablespoon
LEMON JUICE, fresh	1/4 cup
DILL WEED	1-1/2 teaspoons
PARSLEY, chopped	as needed

FILLET OF HADDOCK BAKED IN TOMATO SHELLS

Yield: 24 portions

Ingredients

TOMATOES, RIPE, 3-INCH SIZE	12
SALT	as needed
HADDOCK FILLETS, 5-OUNCE	24
PEPPER	as needed
TOMATO SOUP, CONDENSED	1 50-ounce can
OLIVES, RIPE, PITTED	12
PARSLEY, chopped	as needed

Procedure

1. Cut tomatoes in half. Carefully scoop out flesh and seeds to make uncut shells. Sprinkle shells with salt.
2. Season haddock fillets with salt and pepper. Roll up fillets, starting at wider end. Place each roll in a tomato shell.
3. Place tomatoes on oiled baking sheets. Bake in oven at 375°F. for 5 minutes.
4. Baste each fish roll with the undiluted soup, allowing about 1/4 cup per portion. Bake 10 minutes longer or until fish and tomato are done.
5. Garnish with half a ripe olive and a sprinkle of parsley.

Procedure

1. Place portioned pieces of haddock in shallow pans, one layer deep. Sprinkle lightly with salt and lemon juice. Add water to depth of 1/4 inch.
2. Cover pans; bake in oven at 350°F. for 20 to 30 minutes or until fish flakes easily when tested with a fork.
3. Drain fish. Chill.
4. Combine mayonnaise, wine, lemon rind, lemon juice, and dill. Chill well to blend flavors.
5. Serve chilled fish with sauce spooned over. Garnish with chopped parsley.

BAKED FISH IN CREOLE SAUCE

Yield: 48 portions, 4 ounces fish, 2 ounces sauce

Ingredients	
HADDOCK FILLETS	12 pounds
FLOUR	2 cups
ONION, chopped	2 cups
GREEN PEPPER, chopped	2 cups
SHORTENING	4 tablespoons
SALT	6 tablespoons
PEPPER	1 tablespoon
TOMATOES	2 quarts
TOMATO SOUP	2 quarts
LEMONS, thinly sliced	2

Procedure

1. Cut fish into serving-sized pieces; coat lightly with flour. Arrange in 3 greased steam table pans.
2. Cook onion and green pepper in shortening until tender.
3. Add salt and pepper. Blend in tomatoes and tomato soup.
4. Pour sauce over fish. Distribute lemon slices over top.
5. Bake in oven at 375°F. for 45 minutes.

SCANDINAVIAN FISH PUDDING

(See picture, page 199)

Yield: 16 portions

Ingredients

HADDOCK or COD FILLETS, cut into small pieces	1-1/2 pounds
MILK	1 quart
EGGS	4
CORNSTARCH	1/2 cup
SALT	2 teaspoons
WHITE PEPPER	1/2 teaspoon
BUTTER, soft	4 ounces
PEAS, TINY, FROZEN, cooked	1 quart
WHITE SAUCE, MEDIUM	1 quart
NUTMEG	1 teaspoon
SHRIMP, SMALL, cooked	2 pounds

Procedure

1. Combine fish and milk in 1-gallon food blender. Cover; blend 10 seconds at low speed. Scrape down; blend another 10 seconds.
2. Add eggs, cornstarch, salt, pepper, and butter; blend together at low speed 10 seconds.
3. Pour into well-buttered 2-quart ring mold or into two 1-quart molds.
4. Set mold in pan of warm water. Bake in oven at 350°F. for 1-1/4 to 1-1/2 hours, or until set.
5. Remove from oven; allow to set for 10 minutes.
6. Unmold onto serving platter; mound hot cooked peas in center.
7. Season white sauce with nutmeg. Add shrimp; heat through.
8. Pour sauce around top and edges of mold or serve sauce on side.

BROILED HALIBUT STEAK PIQUANT

Yield: 48 portions

Ingredients

OIL or SHORTENING, melted	2 cups
SALT	3 tablespoons
INSTANT ONION POWDER	1 teaspoon
PAPRIKA	1 teaspoon
BLACK PEPPER	1 teaspoon
HALIBUT STEAKS, 6- to 7-OUNCE	48

Procedure

1. Mix oil, salt, onion powder, paprika, and pepper.
2. Dip fish in oil mixture. Broil until done, turning once during cooking.
3. Serve with Piquant Sauce.*

Note

For best results, cook fish to order.

*PIQUANT SAUCE

Yield: 48 portions

Ingredients

DRY MUSTARD	1 tablespoon
WATER, warm	1 tablespoon
BUTTER, melted and clarified	2 cups
LEMON JUICE	1/4 cup
PARSLEY FLAKES	1/4 cup
INSTANT GARLIC POWDER	1 teaspoon

Procedure

1. Mix mustard with warm water; let stand 10 minutes for flavor to develop.
2. Combine mustard with remaining ingredients; mix well.
3. Spoon sauce over broiled fish allowing approximately 2 teaspoons per portion.

DIETER'S DEVILED HALIBUT

Yield: 24 portions

Ingredients

HALIBUT STEAKS, FRESH or FROZEN, 5-OUNCE	7-1/2 pounds
PREPARED MUSTARD	1/3 cup
COOKING OIL	2 tablespoons
CHILI SAUCE	1/3 cup
HORSERADISH	1/3 cup
SALT	1 teaspoon

SOUTHERN BAKED HALIBUT

Yield: 25 portions

Ingredients

HALIBUT STEAKS, FRESH or FROZEN, 4- to 6-OUNCE	25
ORANGE RIND, grated	2 tablespoons plus 2 teaspoons
SALT	4 teaspoons
NUTMEG	1-1/2 teaspoons
BUTTER or MARGARINE	8 ounces
ORANGE JUICE	3/4 cup

Procedure

1. Thaw frozen fish. Place in a single layer in well-greased baking pans.
2. Cream orange rind, salt, and nutmeg with butter. Gradually add orange juice, beating until blended.
3. Cover fish with the sauce. Bake in oven at 350°F. for 30 to 40 minutes or until fish flakes easily when tested with a fork.

Procedure

1. Thaw fish, if frozen.
2. Combine mustard, oil, chili sauce, horseradish, and salt.
3. Place fish on lightly greased broiler rack. Broil under medium heat about 6 minutes.
4. Turn fish; spread with sauce. Broil 5 to 6 minutes longer or until done.

HALIBUT HAWAIIAN

Yield: 100 portions, 3 quarts basting sauce

Ingredients

SOY SAUCE, JAPANESE	1 quart
PINEAPPLE JUICE	2 cups
SYRUP from CANNED PEACHES	2 cups
WATER	1 quart
VINEGAR	1-1/2 cups
SUGAR	3 pounds
GARLIC	3 cloves
GINGER, GROUND	2 teaspoons
HALIBUT FILLETS or STEAKS	100

Procedure

1. Mix soy sauce, fruit juices, water, and vinegar. Add sugar; stir until dissolved.
2. Mash garlic. Combine with ginger; add to soy sauce mixture.
3. Simmer 20 minutes. Strain. Store until needed.
4. Panfry halibut on both sides, basting liberally with sauce.

HALIBUT CACCIATORE

Yield: 48 portions

Ingredients

ONION FLAKES	2-2/3 cups
SWEET PEPPER FLAKES	1 cup
INSTANT MINCED GARLIC	2 tablespoons
WATER	2-2/3 cups
HALIBUT, cut into 2-inch chunks	16 pounds
FLOUR	2 cups
COOKING OIL	2 cups
COOKING OIL	1/2 cup
TOMATOES, broken up	2 No. 10 cans
OREGANO LEAVES	2-1/2 tablespoons
SALT	2-1/2 tablespoons
BLACK PEPPER, GROUND	1 teaspoon
MUSHROOMS, sliced	2 pounds

Procedure

1. Rehydrate onion flakes, sweet pepper flakes, and minced garlic in water for 10 minutes.
2. Dredge halibut in flour; shake off excess.
3, Brown fish in first amount of oil in a skillet until golden. Remove fish; set aside.
4. Add remaining oil to skillet; heat. Add onion, sweet pepper, and garlic; saute 3 minutes.
5. Combine with tomatoes, oregano, salt, and pepper. Simmer, uncovered, for 10 minutes.
6. Add mushrooms and browned fish. Cover; simmer 10 minutes longer or until fish flakes when tested with a fork.
7. Serve with spaghetti, if desired.

NORTH PACIFIC HALIBUT POLYNESIAN EN CASSEROLE ON CHINESE NOODLES

Yield: 48 portions

Ingredients

HALIBUT FLITCH or STEAK, cut into cubes	9 pounds
ONION, chopped	2 quarts
CELERY, sliced	2 quarts
GREEN PEPPER, chopped	1 quart
MUSHROOMS, sliced	2 cups
PEANUT OIL	as needed
STOCK	1-1/2 quarts
SOY SAUCE	1/2 cup
CORNSTARCH	1/2 cup
WATER, cold	1/2 cup
WATER CHESTNUTS, sliced	2 cups
PINEAPPLE CHUNKS, drained	1 quart
PIMIENTO, chopped	2 cups
CHINESE NOODLES, FRIED	2 gallons

Procedure

1. Poach halibut cubes; drain.
2. Saute onion, celery, green pepper, and mushrooms in oil. Add stock and soy sauce.
3. Blend cornstarch and cold water; stir into mixture. Cook and stir until thickened and clear.
4. Add halibut, water chestnuts, pineapple, and pimiento; heat through.
5. Serve over noodles in individual casseroles.

BAKED HALIBUT, PARSLEY BUTTER SAUCE ➤

Yield: 160 4-ounce portions

Ingredients	
HALIBUT, FROZEN	40 pounds
SALT	1/2 cup
PEPPER	2 tablespoons
FLOUR	2 pounds
LEMON JUICE	2 cups
BUTTER, melted	4 pounds
PARSLEY, chopped	3 cups

ESCALLOPED HALIBUT AND SHRIMP

Yield: 30 6-ounce portions

Ingredients	
HALIBUT	6 pounds
SALT	2 tablespoons
PEPPERCORNS, WHOLE	1 tablespoon
ONION, sliced	1/2 pound
BAY LEAVES	6
SHRIMP, peeled and deveined	2 pounds
EGGS, hard-cooked, sliced	6
WHITE SAUCE, MEDIUM	2-1/2 quarts
BREAD CRUMBS, buttered	as needed

Procedure

1. Poach halibut in water with salt, peppercorns, onion, and bay leaves until fish flakes easily but is still moist.
2. Cook shrimp in salted water, to which a few slices of onion have been added, until shrimp is pink.
3. Remove halibut from bones, and flake.
4. Place alternate layers of halibut, hard-cooked eggs, and shrimp in two 12-inch by 20- inch counter pans.
5. Divide sauce equally between pans.
6. Cover each pan with buttered crumbs and bake in oven at 350°F. until crumbs are brown.

Procedure

1. Thaw fish; cut in 4-ounce portions.
2. Mix salt and pepper with flour.
3. Dip fish in seasoned flour. Place in greased steam table pans.
4. Bake in oven at 350°F. for 15 minutes.
5. Remove from oven; pour lemon juice and butter over fish. Return to oven; bake an additional 15 minutes.
6. Sprinkle with parsley just before serving.

HALIBUT STEAKS, WORCESTERSHIRE BUTTER SAUCE

Yield: 48 portions

Ingredients	
HALIBUT STEAKS, 5-OUNCE	48
COOKING OIL	3/4 cup
SALT	2-1/2 tablespoons
PAPRIKA	4 teaspoons
BUTTER or MARGARINE, clarified	2 pounds
LEMON JUICE	1 cup
WORCESTERSHIRE SAUCE	1/4 cup
SALT	as needed
PARSLEY, finely chopped	1/2 cup

Procedure

1. Prepare fish to order as needed. Lightly brush both sides of fish steaks with oil.
2. Mix first amount of salt and paprika.
3. Sprinkle one side of fish steaks with mixture; broil about 5 minutes. Turn fish; sprinkle again with salt mixture. Broil 5 minutes longer or until just done. Place on warm platter.
4. Prepare sauce tableside. Place skillet or pan over heater. For 2 portions, put 2-1/2 tablespoons butter, 2 teaspoons lemon juice, 1/2 teaspoon Worcestershire sauce, and a dash of salt in pan. Sprinkle with 1 teaspoon parsley. Heat thoroughly.
5. Place 2 broiled fish steaks in sauce. Heat through. Serve with lemon slices, if desired.

BAKED FLOUNDER FILLETS FLORENTINE

Yield: 16 portions

Ingredients	
ONION, chopped	1/2 cup
SHORTENING	1/4 cup
MUSHROOMS, drained, chopped	1 8-ounce can
SPINACH, cooked, chopped	3 cups (1 pound, 14 ounces)
FLOUNDER FILLETS	4 pounds (16 4-ounce portions)
WATER	2 quarts
THYME	1/4 teaspoon
PEPPER	1/4 teaspoon
LEMON JUICE	1 tablespoon
CREAM of CELERY SOUP, CONDENSED	1 50-ounce can
FISH STOCK	1 cup
CHEESE, CHEDDAR, shredded	8 ounces
BREAD CRUMBS, buttered	3/4 cup
PAPRIKA	as needed

Procedure

1. Saute onion in shortening until transparent. Add mushrooms and spinach.
2. Using No. 16 scoop, space 16 mounds of the mixture in 12-inch by 18-inch by 2-inch baking pan.
3. Poach fish in water seasoned with thyme and pepper 6 to 8 minutes; drain, reserving required amount of stock.
4. Top spinach with poached fish; sprinkle with lemon juice.
5. Blend soup and fish stock; stir in cheese. Pour over fish.
6. Sprinkle with crumbs and paprika.
7. Bake in oven at 450°F. for about 20 minutes or until sauce bubbles and crumbs are browned.

Note

For individual casseroles, top each portion with 1/2 cup sauce. Bake in oven at 450°F. for 10 minutes.

ORANGE FISH ROLLS

Yield: 25 portions

Ingredients

ORANGES	4
CELERY, chopped	1 cup
ONION, finely chopped	1/4 cup
BUTTER or MARGARINE	4 ounces
BREAD CRUMBS, seasoned	2 cups
MONOSODIUM GLUTAMATE	4 teaspoons
SALT	2 teaspoons
FLOUNDER FILLETS, 5-1/2-OUNCE	25
SUGAR	4 teaspoons
SALT	2 teaspoons
GINGER, GROUND	1 teaspoon
DRY MUSTARD	1 teaspoon
CORNSTARCH	1/4 cup
ORANGE JUICE	2 quarts

Procedure

1. Grate rind of oranges. Peel oranges; section; dice segments.
2. Saute celery and onion in butter until tender.
3. Add bread crumbs and diced oranges; mix lightly.
4. Sprinkle fillets with monosodium glutamate and first amount of salt. Spread crumb mixture on fillets. Roll up, beginning at large end; fasten with wooden pick.
5. Combine sugar, remaining salt, ginger, mustard, cornstarch, and grated orange rind. Add orange juice; bring to a boil.
6. Pour sauce over fish rolls. Cover; simmer 5 to 8 minutes or until fish flakes easily when tested with a fork. Or, bake, covered, in oven at 325°F. for 30 minutes.

HERB-STUFFED FILLET OF FLOUNDER WITH WHITE CLAM SAUCE

Yield: 50 portions

Ingredients

PACKAGED HERB STUFFING	2-1/2 pounds
INSTANT MINCED ONION	3 ounces
CLAM BROTH	1-1/2 quarts
BUTTER or MARGARINE, melted	1/2 pound
LIQUID HOT PEPPER SEASONING	1 teaspoon
FLOUNDER FILLETS, 4-OUNCE	100
SALT	as needed
BUTTER or MARGARINE, melted	1/2 pound
SALT	as needed
PAPRIKA	as needed

Procedure

1. Combine stuffing, onion, clam broth, first amount of melted butter, and liquid hot pepper seasoning.
2. Arrange half of the fillets side by side on greased sheetpans. Sprinkle with salt.
3. Spread 3 ounces stuffing mixture over each fillet.
4. Top with remaining fillets.
5. Drizzle with remaining melted butter. Sprinkle with salt and paprika.
6. Bake in oven at 325°F. for 20 minutes or until fish flakes easily when tested with a fork. Serve with White Clam Sauce.*

*Recipe on facing page.

*WHITE CLAM SAUCE

Yield: 50 portions

Ingredients

BUTTER or MARGARINE	1/2 pound
FLOUR	1/2 pound
CLAM BROTH	3 quarts
CLAMS, CHOPPED, CANNED	2 pounds
LIQUID HOT PEPPER SEASONING	1 teaspoon
SALT	as needed
MONOSODIUM GLUTAMATE	as needed

Procedure

1. Melt butter; blend in flour.
2. Add clam broth; cook and stir until thickened and smooth. Add clams and liquid hot pepper seasoning.
3. Correct seasoning with salt and monosodium glutamate.

Red Snapper Florida *(Recipe, following page)*

Cling Peach Advisory Board

RED SNAPPER FLORIDA

(See picture, preceding page)

Yield: 40 portions

Ingredients

CLING PEACH SLICES	1 No. 10 can
CREAM	1-1/4 quarts
SALT	2 tablespoons
PEPPER	1 teaspoon
RED SNAPPER FILLETS, 6-OUNCE	40
FLOUR	as needed
SEASONED EGG BATTER	as needed
BUTTER or MARGARINE, melted	1-1/2 pounds
WORCESTERSHIRE SAUCE	1/2 cup
LEMON JUICE	1/2 cup
ALMONDS, BLANCHED, SLICED	2 cups
BUTTER or MARGARINE	4 ounces
PARSLEY SPRIGS	40
LEMON WEDGES	40
SPINACH-STUFFED TOMATO HALVES	40

Procedure

1. Drain peaches; dice.
2. Combine cream, salt, and pepper. Pour over fish; marinate about 1/2 hour.
3. Drain fish. Coat pieces with flour. Dip in batter.
4. Saute or fry until golden brown and fish is done.
5. Combine melted butter, Worcestershire, and lemon juice. Dress fish with mixture; keep warm.
6. Saute almonds in remaining butter until golden. Add diced peaches; heat through.
7. Spoon about 1-1/2 ounces peach sauce over each portion of fish. Garnish plates with parsley and lemon. Serve with spinach-stuffed tomatoes.

SALMON STEAKS WITH GRAPEFRUIT

Yield: 24 portions

Ingredients

ONIONS, SMALL, thinly sliced	6
BUTTER or MARGARINE	1/2 pound
BREAD CRUMBS, soft	1 quart
SALT	2 teaspoons
PEPPER	1/2 teaspoon
ALLSPICE	1/2 teaspoon
SALMON STEAKS	24
GRAPEFRUIT JUICE	1-1/2 cups
GRAPEFRUIT SECTIONS, FRESH, READY-TO-SERVE, drained	1-1/2 quarts
BUTTER or MARGARINE, melted	1/2 pound
PARSLEY	as needed

Procedure

1. Lightly saute onions in first amount of butter; stir in crumbs and seasonings. Remove from heat.

2. Arrange salmon steaks in well-buttered baking pan or individual baking dishes.

3. Pour grapefruit juice over fish. Spread crumb mixture evenly over fish.

4. Bake in oven at 450°F. for 10 minutes. Remove from oven. Reset oven for 375°F.

5. Arrange grapefruit sections on top of fish; baste with melted butter. Continue baking, basting frequently, 15 minutes or until browned and fish flakes easily when tested with a fork. Garnish with parsley.

POACHED SALMON

Yield: approximately 20 portions

Ingredients	
WHITE WINE	1 bottle (4/5 quart)
WATER	1 quart
LEMON JUICE	2 tablespoons
CELERY and CELERY TOPS	4 ounces
ONION, sliced	8 ounces
PARSLEY	1 ounce
SALT	2 tablespoons
BAY LEAVES	3
PEPPERCORNS, WHOLE	1 teaspoon
THYME	1 teaspoon
SALMON, FRESH	10 pounds

Procedure

1. Combine wine, water, lemon juice, vegetables, and seasonings. Bring to a boil. Reduce heat; simmer 30 minutes. Strain.
2. Measure salmon at thickest part. Place fish on a flat, oiled poacher tray or wrap in cheesecloth. Place in poacher (or pot if poacher is unavailable).
3. Add hot liquid, completely covering fish with liquid.
4. Simmer, allowing 10 minutes per measured inch or until fish flakes when tested with a fork. (Fish may be turned after half of cooking time.)
5. Remove fish from liquid to avoid overcooking. Cool slightly.
6. Remove cheesecloth, if used. Remove skin from fish. Chill.
7. Garnish with aspic, if desired. Serve with Remoulade or Sour Cream Dill Sauce.

COLD SALMON WITH ALMONDS AND GUACAMOLE

Yield: 12 portions

Ingredients

SALMON STEAKS, FROZEN, 6-OUNCE	12
SALT	as needed
PEPPER	as needed
BUTTER or MARGARINE, melted	2 ounces (1/4 cup)
DRY VERMOUTH	4 ounces (1/2 cup)
ALMONDS, SLIVERED, toasted	1-1/2 cups
GUACAMOLE, FRESH or FROZEN, thawed	3 cups
SOUR CREAM	2 cups
WATERCRESS	as needed
CHERRY TOMATOES	12

Procedure

1. Place frozen salmon in single layer in shallow baking pan. Sprinkle with salt and pepper.
2. Combine butter and vermouth; pour over salmon.
3. Cover pan. Bake in oven at 400°F. for 40 minutes or until fish is done. Chill salmon in the liquid in pan.
4. Mix half the almonds with the guacamole.
5. To serve, spoon about 1/4 cup of the guacamole mixture on each salmon steak. Spoon a generous tablespoon of sour cream on top. Sprinkle with 1 tablespoon almonds.
6. Garnish with watercress and a cherry tomato. Accompany with hot parsley-buttered potatoes, if desired.

FILLETS DE SOLE DE LA MANCHE AU CHABLIS

Yield: 2 portions

Ingredients

DOVER SOLE FILLETS	4
MUSHROOMS, FRESH	4 large
BUTTER	4 ounces
LEMON JUICE	few drops
SHALLOTS, chopped	1/2 teaspoon
SALT	as needed
PEPPER	as needed
CHABLIS WINE (WHITE)	1/4 bottle
FISH STOCK	3 ounces
LEMON JUICE from	1 lemon
CREAM, HEAVY	6 ounces
TRUFFLE	4 slices
FISH GLACE (reduced fish stock)	1/2 ounce
FLEURONS	4 pieces

Procedure

1. Trim fillets of sole.
2. Sculpture mushrooms; cook slowly in butter as needed, adding a few drops of lemon juice to retain whiteness. Chop stems of mushrooms.
3. Place shallots, mushroom stems, and seasonings in a baking dish. Arrange sole on top. Moisten with Chablis, fish stock and lemon juice. Add salt and pepper.
4. Poach slowly in oven about 12 minutes.
5. Remove sole. Reduce cooking sauce, adding heavy cream until obtaining consistency desired. Strain sauce through a muslin. Add remaining butter, stirring constantly over high heat.
6. Arrange fillets on a large plate. Garnish each with a mushroom cap; cover with prepared sauce. Garnish mushrooms with a slice of truffle.
7. Finish with a lacing of fish glace around the fillets and 4 pieces of fleurons to finish the decoration.

STUFFED SOLE IMPERIAL

Yield: 1 portion

Ingredients

SOLE FILLET, 10-OUNCE	1
CRAB STUFFING*	2 ounces
BUTTER	as needed

Procedure

1. Make a 2-inch cut in sole. Using boning knife, make a pocket 1 inch deep on both sides of cut.
2. Fill with crab stuffing. Saute in butter, cut side up, 8 minutes.
3. Place under broiler to finish cooking (about 10 minutes).

*CRAB STUFFING

Yield: 3 quarts

Ingredients

MAYONNAISE	3/4 cup
EGG YOLKS	4
RED PEPPER	1/2 teaspoon
DRY MUSTARD	2 tablespoons
MONOSODIUM GLUTAMATE	1/2 teaspoon
SALT	1/2 teaspoon
CRABMEAT	3 pounds
GREEN PEPPER, diced	1 medium
PIMIENTO, diced	1

Procedure

1. Combine mayonnaise and egg yolks.
2. Add seasonings. Toss with crabmeat, green pepper, and diced pimiento.

SOLE SUMMER STYLE →

Yield: 12 portions

Ingredients

SOLE FILLETS, FROZEN, 3-OUNCE	24
SALT	as needed
PEPPER	as needed
GREEN ONIONS, finely chopped	3/4 cup
DILL WEED	1 tablespoon
LEMON JUICE	1/4 cup
TOMATO SLICES	12
CHEESE, CHEDDAR, SHARP, grated	6 ounces (1-1/2 cups)
ALMONDS, UNBLANCHED, chopped	4-1/2 ounces (1 cup)

SOLE A LA BONNE FEMME

Yield: 24 portions

Ingredients

SOLE FILLETS, FROZEN	8 to 10 pounds
MUSHROOMS, sliced	1-1/2 quarts
SHALLOTS, minced	6
PARSLEY, chopped	1/3 cup
DRY WHITE WINE	1 quart
CREAM SAUCE, THICK, warm	2-1/2 quarts
NUTMEG	dash

Procedure

1. Thaw fillets. Dry with paper toweling or damp cloth.
2. Arrange fillets in single layer in oiled baking pans. Cover with mushrooms, shallots, and parsley. Pour wine into pans.
3. Cover lightly with heavy paper. Bake in oven at 350°F. for 25 to 30 minutes, or until fish flakes easily when tested with fork.
4. With bulb baster, draw up liquid from baking pans; strain into saucepan. Boil until amount of liquid is reduced to approximately 1/2 its volume.
5. Stir liquid into warm cream sauce. Add nutmeg.
6. Spoon sauce over fillets; run under broiler until sauce is delicately browned.

Procedure

1. Place frozen sole in shallow pan, overlapping fillets in pairs. Sprinkle with salt and pepper.
2. Sprinkle fish with green onion, dill weed, and lemon juice.
3. Top each portion with a tomato slice.
4. Combine cheese and almonds; sprinkle over fish and tomato.
5. Bake, uncovered, in oven at 400°F. for 25 minutes or until fish is done.

FILLET OF SOLE, FLORENTINE

Yield: 1 portion

Ingredients

EGG, hard-cooked, sliced	1
SPINACH, cooked, drained, chopped	1/2 cup
MUSHROOMS, sliced, sauteed	1 tablespoon
SOLE FILLET, rolled, poached	1
MORNAY SAUCE	2 ounces

Procedure

1. Have all ingredients hot. Arrange slices of egg around sides of a warm individual casserole. Place spinach in bottom of dish; sprinkle with mushrooms.
2. Arrange fillet on spinach; ladle sauce on top.
3. Place under broiler a few minutes, until thoroughly hot.

FILLET OF SOLE TULLAMORE

Yield: 1 portion

Ingredients

SOLE FILLET	8 ounces
SALT	as needed
PEPPER	as needed
BUTTER, melted	2 ounces
SHERRY WINE	1 ounce
SHRIMP SAUCE*	2 ounces

Procedure

1. Season sole with salt and pepper. Combine butter and sherry; sprinkle over fish.
2. Broil or pan saute until fish flakes easily when tested with a fork. Remove to serving plate; cover with sauce.

*SHRIMP SAUCE

Yield: approximately 1-1/8 gallons

Ingredients

WHITE SAUCE, MEDIUM	1 gallon
PAPRIKA	3 tablespoons
ALASKA SHRIMP, cooked	1 pound
SHERRY WINE	1/2 cup
MUSHROOMS, CANNED, SLICED	1/2 cup
ONION, very finely chopped	1 tablespoon
SALT	as needed
PEPPER	as needed
MONOSODIUM GLUTAMATE	as needed

Procedure

1. Combine white sauce, paprika, cooked shrimp, sherry, mushrooms, and onion. Add salt, pepper, and monosodium glutamate to taste.
2. Blend thoroughly; heat.

SHRIMP-FILLED SOLE

Yield: 18 portions

Ingredients

MUSHROOMS, STEMS and PIECES, drained	3/4 cup
BUTTER	2 ounces
SHRIMP, SMALL, cooked	2 cups
SALT	2 teaspoons
PEPPER	1/2 teaspoon
ONION, finely chopped	1/2 cup
SOLE FILLETS, 5-OUNCE	18
CREAM of MUSHROOM SOUP, CONDENSED, UNDILUTED	1 quart
CHEESE, SHARP, grated	1-1/2 cups

Procedure

1. Saute mushrooms in butter. Add shrimp, seasonings, and onion.
2. Spread shrimp mixture over fish fillets. Roll; fasten with toothpicks. Place rolls in large shallow baking pan.
3. Pour soup over fillets. Sprinkle with cheese.
4. Bake in oven at 400°F. for 20 minutes or until fish flakes when tested with a fork.

Fish Almondine, Mushroom Sauce Gourmet

California Blue Diamond Almond Growers Exchange; Cling Peach Advisory Board

HERB-STUFFED FISH ROLLUPS

Yield: 50 portions

Ingredients

ONION, finely chopped	1 cup
BUTTER or MARGARINE, melted	3/4 pound
RICE, cooked	2 quarts
SALT	1 tablespoon
PEPPER	1/2 teaspoon
PAPRIKA	2 teaspoons
BASIL	1 tablespoon
DILL WEED	1/2 tablespoon
LEMON JUICE	6 tablespoons
BREAD CRUMBS, dried	1-1/2 cups
SOLE or FLOUNDER FILLETS	12-1/2 pounds
BUTTER or MARGARINE, melted	3/4 pound
WATER	1 cup
SALT	1 tablespoon
PAPRIKA	1 teaspoon

Procedure

1. Cook onion in butter until soft. Remove from heat. Add rice, seasonings, lemon juice, and crumbs; mix thoroughly.

2. Cut fillets into 4-ounce portions. If necessary, put several pieces together. A meat mallet may be used to flatten fish. Use a No. 30 scoop for portioning stuffing on each fillet; roll up lengthwise.

3. Place fillets, open edge down, about 1 inch apart on greased shallow baking pan. Drizzle melted butter and water over fish rollups. Sprinkle with salt and paprika.

4. Bake in oven at 400°F. for 20 to 30 minutes or until fish flakes easily when tested with a fork and is lightly browned. Baste with the drippings.

Note

After removing from oven, cover fish to prevent drying.

SOLE VALENCIA

Yield: 48 portions

Ingredients

ONION FLAKES	2 cups
SWEET PEPPER FLAKES	3/4 cup
INSTANT MINCED GARLIC	1-1/2 teaspoons
WATER	2 cups
OLIVE or SALAD OIL	3/4 cup
TOMATOES, broken up	1 No. 10 can
TOMATO SAUCE	1-1/2 quarts
BAY LEAVES	5
SAFFRON, WHOLE, crumbled	1 teaspoon
FLOUR	1-1/4 cups
BREAD CRUMBS, dry	1-1/4 cups
SALT	3 tablespoons
BLACK PEPPER, GROUND	1-1/2 teaspoons
SOLE FILLET	48 portions (12 pounds)
OLIVE or SALAD OIL	as needed

Procedure

1. Combine onion, sweet pepper flakes, and minced garlic; rehydrate in water for 10 minutes.

2. Saute vegetable mixture in first amount of oil in a saucepan 5 minutes.

3. Add tomatoes, tomato sauce, bay leaves, and saffron. Cook, stirring occasionally, for 10 minutes.

4. Combine flour, crumbs, salt, and pepper. Dredge fish in mixture. Panfry in skillet, using 1/4-inch depth of oil.

5. Spoon sauce over fish for service.

ORANGE-RICE STUFFED RAINBOW TROUT →

Yield: 25 portions

Ingredients	
RAINBOW TROUT, 8-OUNCE, PAN-DRESSED, FRESH or FROZEN	25
SALT	3 tablespoons
ORANGE-RICE STUFFING*	5-1/4 pounds
OIL or SHORTENING, melted	1/2 cup
ORANGE JUICE	1/2 cup
PAPRIKA	1 tablespoon

*ORANGE-RICE STUFFING

Yield: 25 portions

Ingredients	
WATER	2-1/2 cups
ORANGE JUICE	1 cup
LEMON JUICE	1/2 cup
ORANGE RIND, grated	1/4 cup
SALT	1 tablespoon
RICE, UNCOOKED	1 pound (2-1/4 cups)
CELERY, chopped	1 quart
ONION, chopped	1 cup
OIL or SHORTENING, melted	1/2 cup
ALMONDS, SLIVERED, toasted	2 cups
PARSLEY, chopped	1/2 cup

Procedure

1. Combine water, juices, orange rind, and salt; bring to a boil.
2. Place rice in a 12-inch by 10-inch by 2-inch baking pan. Pour boiling liquid over rice. Stir to distribute evenly in pan.
3. Cover tightly. Bake in oven at 350°F. for 45 to 60 minutes or until tender. Remove from oven. Let stand 5 minutes.
4. Saute celery and onion in oil until tender but not brown.
5. Combine rice, vegetables, almonds, and parsley. Toss lightly to mix.

Procedure

1. Thaw frozen fish. Clean, wash, and dry fish.
2. Sprinkle fish with salt, inside and out.
3. Portion stuffing with a No. 10 scoop. Stuff fish.
4. Place fish, cut edge down, on well-greased sheetpans.
5. Combine oil and orange juice. Brush fish with mixture. Sprinkle with paprika.
6. Bake in oven at 350°F. for 35 to 45 minutes or until fish flakes easily when tested with a fork.

BROILED TROUT WITH MUSHROOM SAUCE

Yield: 15 portions, 1-1/4 quarts sauce

Ingredients

MUSHROOMS, FRESH, sliced	6
BUTTER	3 ounces
FLOUR	6 tablespoons
CHICKEN BOUILLON	1 quart
TOMATO SAUCE	1 cup
SHERRY WINE	1/3 cup
PARSLEY, chopped	1/3 cup
DILL	1/4 teaspoon
POULTRY SEASONING	1/4 teaspoon
RAINBOW TROUT, 5-OUNCE	15
SALT	as needed
BUTTER, melted	as needed

Procedure

1. Saute mushrooms in butter; blend in flour; brown.
2. Add bouillon, tomato sauce, sherry, parsley, and seasonings; simmer 1/2 hour.
3. Salt trout lightly. Broil, basting with melted butter.
4. Ladle 1/4 to 1/3 cup sauce over each trout. Serve with buttered noodles seasoned with chopped chives.

BONED RAINBOW TROUT, TOWERS STYLE ➔

Yield: 6 portions

Ingredients	
CONTINENTAL TROUT, 6-OUNCE, BONED	6
SALT	as needed
WHITE PEPPER	as needed
PAPRIKA	as needed
WILD RICE, cooked	2 ounces
BROWN RICE, cooked	2 ounces
TOMATO SLICES, 1/4-inch thick	6
MUSHROOM CAPS, LARGE	6
GRAPES, WHITE, SEEDLESS	30
SHRIMP (15 to pound)	12
BUTTER, melted	as needed

Fillets, Frutas

Cling Peach Advisory Board

Procedure

1. Place trout in buttered shallow pan. Season with salt, pepper, and paprika.
2. Combine wild and brown rice. Spoon inside trout. Top each fish with a tomato slice, mushroom cap, 5 grapes, and 2 shrimp.
3. Brush with melted butter. Bake in oven at 350°F. until trout is just done, about 20 minutes.
4. Serve with a garnish of lemon, parsley, and green vegetable.

MOUNTAIN TROUT SIERRA

Yield: 2 portions

Ingredients

TROUT, LARGE	2
BUTTER or MARGARINE, melted	2 ounces
SALT	1 teaspoon
PEPPER	1/8 teaspoon
LEMON RIND, grated	1 tablespoon
FLOUR	as needed
BUTTER or MARGARINE	1/2 ounce
LEMON JUICE	1 tablespoon
PARSLEY, chopped	2 tablespoons
LEMON WEDGES	4

Procedure

1. Wipe trout with damp paper toweling.
2. Combine melted butter, salt, pepper, and grated lemon rind.
3. Brush inside of trout with seasoned butter.
4. Flour trout well on both sides.
5. Put remaining seasoned butter into skillet; panfry trout until done, turning once. Remove to serving dish.
6. Melt butter in skillet; add lemon juice. Heat; pour over fish. Sprinkle with parsley. Garnish with lemon wedges.

ROCKY MOUNTAIN RAINBOW TROUT →

Yield: 6 portions

Ingredients

TROUT, PAN-DRESSED	6
COOKING OIL	1 cup
PARSLEY, chopped	1/4 cup
CATSUP	2 tablespoons
WINE VINEGAR	2 tablespoons
GARLIC, finely chopped	2 cloves
BASIL	2 teaspoons
SALT	1 teaspoon
PEPPER	1/4 teaspoon

PAN TROUT SESAME

Yield: 2 portions

Ingredients

TROUT, LARGE	2
BUTTER, melted	2 to 3 ounces
SESAME SEED, toasted	as needed
LEMON JUICE	1 tablespoon
LEMON WEDGES	4

Procedure

1. Pat trout dry with paper toweling.
2. Dip trout in melted butter; roll in sesame seeds, coating both sides.
3. Panfry trout in remaining butter until done, turning once. Remove to serving plate.
4. Add lemon juice to skillet with drippings. Heat; pour over trout. Serve garnished with lemon wedges.

Procedure

1. Thaw fish, if frozen. Clean, wash, and dry fish. Place in a single layer in a shallow pan.
2. Combine remaining ingredients. Pour over fish; let stand 30 minutes, turning once.
3. Remove fish from marinade, reserving marinade for basting.
4. Broil fish on one side, basting twice. Turn carefully. Brush with marinade; broil, basting occasionally, until fish is done. Do not overcook.

RAINBOW TROUT IN CHAMPAGNE

Yield: 12 portions

Ingredients

TROUT, WHOLE, 5-1/3-OUNCE	12
SALT	as needed
PEPPER	as needed
CHAMPAGNE or WHITE WINE	2 cups
LEMON JUICE	6 tablespoons
LEMONS, quartered	6
CREAM, HEAVY	2 cups

Procedure

1. Season trout with salt and pepper. Place in pan.
2. Pour wine, lemon juice, and lemon quarters over trout. Cover; bake in oven at 350°F. for 15 minutes.
3. Pour cream over fish. Place under broiler until sauce is brown, watching closely to avoid burning.

BROILED WHITEFISH WITH SOUFFLE SAUCE

Yield: 50 portions

Ingredients	
WHITEFISH, LAKE TROUT, SOLE or HALIBUT, 5-OUNCE PORTIONS	50
SALT	as needed
PAPRIKA	as needed
BUTTER or MARGARINE, melted	1 pound
LEMON JUICE	1/4 cup
SOUFFLE SAUCE*	recipe amount

Procedure

1. Place fish on well-greased baking sheets. Sprinkle with salt and paprika.
2. Combine melted butter and lemon juice; drizzle over each portion.
3. Broil just until fish flakes easily with a fork, basting once with lemon butter. Remove from broiler.
4. Spread surface with an even layer of souffle sauce; sprinkle with paprika; return to broiler to brown. *Serve at once.*

*SOUFFLE SAUCE

Yield: for 50 portions of fish

Ingredients	
MAYONNAISE	2 quarts
PICKLES, chopped	1 cup
ONION, finely chopped	1/4 cup
PARSLEY, chopped	1/4 cup
CAPERS, chopped	1/4 cup
OLIVES, chopped	2 cups
VINEGAR or LEMON JUICE	1/4 to 1/2 cup
EGG WHITES	3 cups

Procedure

1. Combine mayonnaise, pickles, onion, parsley, capers, and olives. Blend in vinegar or lemon juice.
2. Chill several hours to thoroughly blend flavors.
3. Beat egg whites until stiff but not dry. Fold into mayonnaise mixture.

SMOKED FISH HASH

Yield: 12 portions

Ingredients

WHITEFISH, SMOKED*	2 pounds
BACON, sliced	1/2 pound
POTATOES, RAW, diced	2 quarts
ONION, finely chopped	1/4 cup
PARSLEY, chopped	1/4 cup
PEPPER	1/4 teaspoon
BACON FAT	1/2 to 2/3 cup
WATER	1 cup
PAPRIKA	as needed

*Or other smoked fish

Procedure

1. Remove skin and bones from fish; flake fish.
2. Cook bacon until crisp; drain, reserving bacon fat. Crumble bacon.
3. Combine flaked fish, bacon, potatoes, onion, parsley, and pepper.
4. Pour bacon fat into a large heavy skillet; heat.
5. Place fish mixture in hot fat; spread evenly across skillet. Pour water over top.
6. Cover; cook over moderate heat for 7 to 8 minutes.
7. Turn mixture. Cook, uncovered, 6 to 8 minutes longer or until lightly browned and potatoes are done. Stir occasionally to mix in browned potatoes. Sprinkle with paprika.

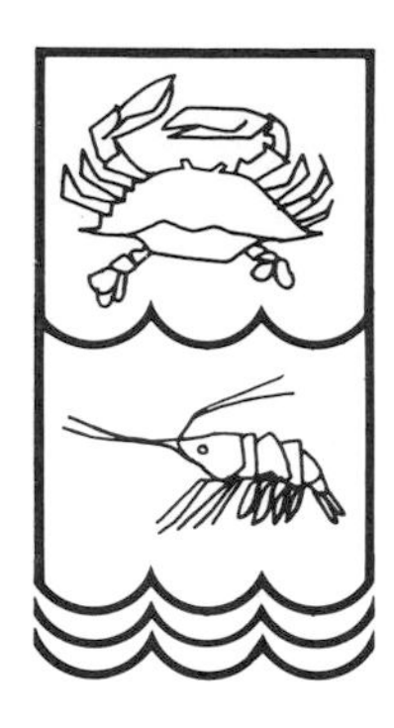

Seafood Entrees

Shrimp Rarebit

Shrimp Assn. of the Americas

Crab

CRABS ARE OTHER members of the shellfish family that appear in a variety of types. The Blue Crab is native to the East Coast, the Dungeness to the Pacific, and the King or Alaska Crab comes from the deep waters of the north Pacific. In addition, there are local types.

Soft shell crabs are not a separate species. They are simply Blue Crab caught during the moulting season after they have shed their old hard shell and before they have grown another (and larger) one. Soft shell crabs are available live and are most plentiful during July and August. This delicacy is also marketed cooked and frozen.

Crabs in the shell can be purchased alive or cooked. The cooked meat picked from the shell comes chilled, canned, or frozen. Canned crab comes as white lump meat, which is considered choice; white flake; a combination of flake and lump; and claw meat which is brownish on the outside.

King crab always comes cooked. Frozen sections in the shell, and frozen and canned meat are the popular forms.

Rice-Stuffed Crab

Rice Council

CRAB SUPREME

Yield: 3 quarts, 24 1/2-cup portions

Ingredients

GREEN PEPPER, diced	2 cups
BUTTER or MARGARINE	2/3 cup
FLOUR	2/3 cup
EGG YOLKS	6
CREAM, LIGHT or HALF-and-HALF	1-3/4 quarts
THYME, LEAVES, DRIED, CRUSHED	1 teaspoon
SALT	2 teaspoons
LEMON JUICE	1/2 cup
CRABMEAT, FRESH, FROZEN, or CANNED	2-3/4 pounds
ALMONDS, SLIVERED, toasted	1/2 cup
AVOCADOS	12
LEMON JUICE	as needed

Procedure

1. Saute green pepper in butter 2 to 3 minutes. Blend in flour.
2. Beat egg yolks with cream; gradually blend into butter mixture. Cook and stir until thickened. Add thyme, salt, and first amount of lemon juice. Remove from heat.
3. Rinse crabmeat; drain. Fold into sauce; heat through gently.
4. Turn into chafing dish insert to keep warm; sprinkle with almonds.
5. Cut avocados lengthwise into halves; remove seeds and skin. Sprinkle with lemon juice.
6. To serve: ladle crab mixture into avocado halves.

CRABMEAT-STUFFED SWEET SPANISH ONIONS

Yield: 48 portions

Ingredients

SWEET SPANISH ONIONS, peeled	48
ONION (from centers), finely chopped	1 cup
MUSHROOMS, finely chopped	1 cup
BUTTER or MARGARINE, melted	4 ounces
KING CRABMEAT	1 pound
PARSLEY, finely chopped	1/4 cup
BREAD CRUMBS	2 cups
WHITE SAUCE, MEDIUM	1 quart
WHITE WINE	1/2 cup
SALT	as needed
CREAM of TOMATO SOUP, CONDENSED	2 50-ounce cans
WATER	1 quart
MARJORAM	1 tablespoon
GARLIC POWDER	1/4 teaspoon
BUTTER or MARGARINE, melted	4 ounces
BREAD CRUMBS	2 cups
CHEESE, grated	6 ounces
KING CRAB LEGS, sliced	3 pounds

Procedure

1. Steam or parboil onions until partially tender. Cool. Remove centers; chop required amount.
2. Saute chopped onion and mushrooms in first amount of butter.
3. Remove from heat. Add crabmeat, parsley, first amount of bread crumbs, cream sauce, and wine. Season with salt.
4. Fill onion shells with crabmeat mixture.
5. Blend soup and water; add marjoram and garlic powder. Pour into baking pans.
6. Place stuffed onions in sauce in pans.
7. Combine remaining butter, bread crumbs, and grated cheese.
8. Top onions with crumb mixture. Cover; bake in oven at 375°F. for 45 minutes. Uncover; continue baking 10 minutes or until topping browns.
9. Garnish portions with slices of crabmeat. Serve with the tomato sauce.

CRAB CAKES I →

Yield: 50 2-ounce cakes

Ingredients

CRABMEAT, flaked	1-1/2 gallons
SALT	1-1/2 tablespoons
WHITE PEPPER	1/2 teaspoon
MONOSODIUM GLUTAMATE	2 teaspoons
DRY MUSTARD	1 tablespoon
PARSLEY, finely chopped	1/2 cup
EGG YOLKS, beaten	12 (1 cup)
MAYONNAISE	3/4 cup
LEMON JUICE	2 tablespoons
BREAD CRUMBS, dry	as needed

CRAB CAKES II

Yield: 100 portions (2 cakes each)

Ingredients

CRABMEAT	24 pounds
BUTTER or MARGARINE	1-1/2 pounds
ONION, finely chopped	3 cups
BREAD CRUMBS, dry	3 quarts
EGGS, well beaten	24
DRY MUSTARD	1/2 cup
SALT	1/4 cup
PEPPER	1 tablespoon
FLOUR	1 pound

Procedure

1. Remove any shell or cartilage from crabmeat.
2. Melt butter; add onion; saute until tender and light brown.
3. Mix crabmeat, onion, bread crumbs, eggs, and seasonings.
4. Shape in small cakes, about 2-1/2 ounces each. Roll in flour.
5. Fry in deep fat at 375°F. for 2 or 3 minutes or until browned. Drain. Serve with parsley cream sauce, if desired.

Procedure

1. Combine crabmeat, seasonings, and parsley; toss lightly.
2. Add egg yolks, mayonnaise, and lemon juice; blend thoroughly.
3. Portion mixture with a No. 16 scoop. Shape into patties.
4. Coat lightly with crumbs. Saute, turning to brown both sides.

CRAB THERMIDOR

Yield: 20 portions

Ingredients

MUSHROOMS, SLICED, drained	2 8-ounce cans
GREEN ONIONS, chopped	1-1/3 cups
BUTTER or MARGARINE	6 ounces
FLOUR	3 ounces (3/4 cup)
DRY MUSTARD	2 teaspoons
HALF-and-HALF or CREAM, LIGHT	1-1/2 quarts
EGG YOLKS, beaten	8 (2/3 cup)
CRABMEAT, drained	4 15-1/2-ounce cans
SALT	as needed
CHEESE, PARMESAN, grated	1-1/3 cups
TOAST POINTS	40

Procedure

1. Cook mushrooms and onions lightly in butter.

2. Blend in flour and mustard. Add 2/3 the amount of half-and-half; cook and stir until thickened.

3. Combine egg yolks with remaining half-and-half; slowly stir into sauce. Continue to cook and stir over low heat 3 to 4 minutes.

4. Add crabmeat. Season with salt; heat through.

5. Turn into ramekins. Sprinkle with cheese; brown under broiler. Serve with toast points.

KING CRAB FOO YUNG

Yield: 48 portions

Ingredients

KING CRABMEAT	2-1/2 pounds
CELERY, finely chopped	1 quart
GREEN ONIONS, finely sliced	1 quart
BEAN SPROUTS, CANNED, drained	2 quarts
MUSHROOMS, CANNED, drained	2 cups
EGGS	48
SOY SAUCE	1/4 cup
PEANUT OIL	as needed
FOO YUNG SAUCE*	3 quarts
RICE, cooked, hot (optional)	2 gallons

Procedure

1. Combine crabmeat and vegetables; toss to mix.
2. Beat eggs until thick; add soy sauce and crabmeat mixture.
3. Portion with a two-ounce ladle into a hot skillet well oiled with peanut oil. Cook until set and lightly browned, turning once.
4. Serve with Foo Yung Sauce and, if desired, rice.

*FOO YUNG SAUCE

Yield: 3 quarts

Ingredients

SUGAR	1/2 cup
CORNSTARCH	1/2 cup
CHICKEN STOCK	3 quarts
SOY SAUCE	3/4 cup
RICE WINE	1/2 cup

Procedure

1. Combine sugar and cornstarch. Add remaining ingredients.
2. Cook and stir until thickened and clear.

SPECIAL KING CRAB PIZZA

Yield: 12 12-inch or 48 6-inch pies

Ingredients

HOT ROLL MIX, prepared for makeup	6 pounds
MAYONNAISE	1-1/2 quarts
SOUR CREAM	1 quart
EGGS	12
LEMON JUICE	1/2 cup
DRY MUSTARD	3 tablespoons
CAYENNE PEPPER	1/2 teaspoon
SALT	2 tablespoons
ONION, chopped	3 cups
GREEN PEPPER, chopped	3 cups
KING CRABMEAT	6 pounds
CHEESE, MOZZARELLA, sliced	3 pounds
CHEESE, PARMESAN, grated	2-1/4 cups

Procedure

1. Divide roll dough into 8-ounce pieces. Line twelve 12-inch pizza pans.
2. Combine mayonnaise, sour cream, eggs, lemon juice, and seasonings; beat until blended.
3. Cover each pizza with 1 cup of sauce, 1/4 cup onion, 1/4 cup green pepper, and 8 ounces crabmeat.
4. Top with 4 ounces mozzarella cheese; sprinkle with 3 tablespoons parmesan cheese.
5. Bake in oven at 400°F. for 15 to 20 minutes or until pizza crust is golden brown and cheese melted.

Variation

For 6-inch pizzas, divide roll dough into 48 2-ounce pieces. Line 48 6-inch baking pans. Cover each pizza with 2 ounces of mayonnaise mixture, 1 tablespoon each of onion and green pepper and 2 ounces crabmeat. Top with a 1-ounce slice of mozzarella cheese and a sprinkling of parmesan. Bake in oven at 400°F. for 15 minutes or until done.

CRAB BISCAYNE →

Yield: 48 1/2-cup portions

Ingredients

CATSUP	3 cups
VINEGAR	3/4 cup
BUTTER or MARGARINE, melted	4 ounces
WORCESTERSHIRE SAUCE	1/4 cup
SALT	1 teaspoon
LIQUID HOT PEPPER SEASONING	1/2 teaspoon
CRABMEAT, flaked	6 pounds
EGGS, hard-cooked, chopped	24
BREAD CRUMBS, soft	1-1/2 quarts
CHEESE, AMERICAN, PROCESSED, grated	1 pound

DEVILED CRAB

Yield: 50 5-ounce portions

Ingredients

CREAM of CELERY SOUP, CONDENSED	3 50-ounce cans
CRABMEAT, flaked	6 pounds
BREAD CRUMBS, dry	1 quart (1 pound)
GREEN PEPPER, diced	1-1/2 cups
ONION, chopped	3/4 cup
LEMON JUICE	3/4 cup
WORCESTERSHIRE SAUCE	1/3 cup
PREPARED MUSTARD	3 tablespoons
LIQUID HOT PEPPER SEASONING	dash
BUTTER or MARGARINE	as needed

Procedure

1. Combine soup, crabmeat, crumbs, green pepper, onion, lemon juice, Worcestershire sauce, mustard, and pepper seasoning; mix lightly.

2. Fill individual shells or pour into three 9-inch by 12-inch by 2-inch baking pans. Dot top with butter.

4. Bake in oven at 350°F., allowing 20 minutes for shells, 1 hour for baking pans.

Procedure

1. Combine catsup, vinegar, butter, Worcestershire, salt, and hot pepper seasoning.
2. Gently mix in crabmeat, eggs, and crumbs.
3. Place mixture in individual shells or casseroles, allowing 1/2-cup mixture per portion. Top with cheese.
4. Bake in oven at 375°F. for 20 minutes or until cheese melts and mixture is hot.

CRABMEAT CHANTILLY

Yield: 20 portions

Ingredients

CRABMEAT	4 pounds
BUTTER or MARGARINE	4 ounces
SHERRY	2 cups
CREAM of CELERY SOUP, CONDENSED	2 quarts
WHITE PEPPER	1/4 teaspoon
SALT	as needed
ASPARAGUS TIPS, FRESH or FROZEN	5 pounds
CREAM, HEAVY, whipped, unsweetened	2 cups
CHEESE, PARMESAN, grated	1 cup

Procedure

1. Saute crabmeat lightly in butter. Add sherry; simmer until liquid is reduced one-half.
2. Add soup and pepper, and salt, if needed. Blend. Heat through.
3. Cook asparagus; drain. Place in well-oiled shallow individual casseroles.
4. Spoon crabmeat mixture over asparagus. Spread whipped cream over crab mixture; sprinkle with cheese. Brown lightly under broiler.

Shrimp Sarapicio *(Recipe, page 196)*

Shrimp Association of the Americas

Frog Legs

FROG LEGS SAUTE

Yield: 25 portions, 4 legs per portion

Ingredients

FROG LEGS	100
BUTTERMILK	1-1/2 quarts
FLOUR	3 cups
BUTTER	1-1/2 cups
SHERRY, DRY	1 cup
MONOSODIUM GLUTAMATE	1-1/2 teaspoons
BUTTER	1-1/2 cups
GARLIC, grated or crushed	2 cloves
PARSLEY, finely chopped	3/4 cup

Procedure

1. Clean frog legs. Arrange in pans and marinate in buttermilk for 1/2 hour.
2. Remove frog legs from buttermilk, roll in flour. Saute in butter until golden brown on both sides, and until juice no longer looks pinkish. (Pierce carefully with fork to check for color.)
3. While legs are still in saute pan, sprinkle with sherry and monosodium glutamate.
4. Serve on hot plates. Heat butter and garlic until slightly browned. Quickly stir in the parsley. While butter is still foaming, spoon over the frog legs. Serve immediately.

Note

Salted butter and monosodium glutamate should provide enough salt.

Stuffed Lobster Tails

Kellogg Company

Lobster

LOBSTERS, THE ARISTOCRATS of the seafood clan, are of two main species. The lobsters native to the northeastern American coast are easily identified by their two large meaty claws. In contrast, the spiny or rock lobsters are practically clawless and carry all of their meat in the tail.

Native lobsters can be purchased alive or boiled and frozen. When bought alive, lobsters should be lively *and show movement of the legs. The "tail" of a healthy live lobster curls under the body and does not hang down when the lobster is picked up.*

Lobster meat, removed from the shell, comes as fresh chilled, frozen, or canned.

The tail section of the rock lobster comes frozen, raw, in the shell. These tail sections are graded for size. There are several kinds on the market with shells of different colors depending on the locality in which they were taken. The meat of the lobster tail should have a clear whitish color.

HEN HOUSE HOMARDS

Yield: 32 hors d'oeuvres

Ingredients

LOBSTER MEAT, FRESH or FROZEN, cooked	1 pound
MAYONNAISE or SALAD DRESSING	2/3 cup
CHILI SAUCE	1 tablespoon
GREEN PEPPER, chopped	1 teaspoon
ONION, grated	1 teaspoon
PIMIENTO, chopped	1 teaspoon
EGGS, hard-cooked	16
PARSLEY	as needed

Procedure

1. Thaw frozen lobster meat; drain. Remove any remaining shell or cartilage. Cut meat into small pieces.
2. Combine mayonnaise, chili sauce, green pepper, onion, and pimiento. Add to lobster; toss lightly to mix.
3. Cut eggs in half lengthwise; remove yolks. (Reserve to use in other recipes.) Fill each white with 1 tablespoon of lobster mixture.
4. Garnish with chopped parsley or parsley sprigs.

LOBSTER TAILS ITALIANO →

Yield: 24 portions

Ingredients

ROCK LOBSTER TAILS, FROZEN, MINIATURE	12 pounds
OLIVE OIL or SALAD OIL	1 cup
SALT	1 tablespoon
WHITE PEPPER	1/2 teaspoon
ITALIAN SEASONING	2 teaspoons
VERMOUTH, EXTRA DRY	1 cup
LEMON JUICE	1/2 cup

SOUTH AFRICAN BUTTERFLY BROIL

Yield: 12 portions

Ingredients

ROCK LOBSTER TAILS, FROZEN, 4-OUNCE	12
CHICKEN BROTH	1 cup
ORANGE JUICE	1/3 cup
LEMON JUICE	3 tablespoons
SOY SAUCE	2 tablespoons
GINGER	1 teaspoon
SALT	1 teaspoon
TARRAGON, DRY	1 teaspoon
GARLIC, crushed	2 cloves
LIQUID HOT PEPPER SEASONING	dash
WHITE WINE, DRY	1/2 cup

Procedure

1. Rinse frozen lobster tails in warm water until slightly thawed.
2. With sharp knife or shears, cut through center of hard shells and meat. Do not clip underside membrane or tail fans.
3. Grasp two halves of cut tail; bend backwards completely to expose flesh.
4. Arrange, flesh side up, in shallow pan.
5. Mix remaining ingredients. Spoon over tails. Marinate for 1 to 2 hours, basting frequently with marinade.
6. Broil, flesh side down, 5 minutes. Turn; baste with marinade; broil flesh side up 5 minutes. Serve at once in shell.

Procedure

1. Thaw lobster tails; remove from shells.
2. Heat oil; add lobster tails and seasonings. Cook 8 to 10 minutes or until lobster is tender, stirring frequently.
3. Increase temperature. Add vermouth and lemon juice. Cook and stir one minute longer. Drain and serve.

STUFFED LOBSTER TAILS, SHERRY BUTTER SAUCE

Yield: 24 portions

Ingredients

LOBSTER TAILS, 1/4-POUND SIZE	48
CREAM of CELERY SOUP, CONDENSED	2 50-ounce cans
ONION SALT	1-1/2 tablespoons
PEPPER	2 teaspoons
PIMIENTO, chopped	1 cup
SHERRY	1 cup
BREAD CRUMBS, coarse, soft, toasted	1 gallon (1-1/2 pounds)
BUTTER, melted	1 cup (8 ounces)
SHERRY	1/2 cup

Procedure

1. Cook lobster tails in salted water according to package directions. Remove meat from shells; dice. Reserve shells.
2. Combine lobster meat with undiluted soup; add onion salt, pepper, pimiento, first amount of sherry, and toasted bread crumbs.
3. Mound mixture into shells. Place filled lobster shells in a 12-inch by 20-inch by 2-1/2-inch steam table pan.
4. Heat in oven at 350°F. for about 20 minutes, or until heated through.
5. Combine butter with remaining sherry. Heat slightly.
6. Allow 2 lobster tails per portion. Pour 1 tablespoon hot sauce over each portion.

Creamed Oysters Over Hot Rice

Rice Council

Oysters

OYSTERS vary in character depending upon the locale from which they come. Some are plump and greyish, others more green than grey, and still others have a coppery cast. Species range in size from very small to as large as the palm of a hand.

Oysters are marketed in their shells and, out of shell (shucked), fresh, frozen, or canned.

Oysters in the shell should be alive. The shells should snap tight when tapped gently. Shucked oysters should be plump, with a natural creamy color and clear liquid.

Avoid shucked oysters with an excess amount of liquid. Liquid is in excess when it totals more than 10 percent by weight of the oysters-in-liquid as taken from the original container. Oysters are sold on a size basis and a difference in price may be due to size rather than quality. Small oysters are usually a better buy for dishes where impressive size is unimportant.

Based on the number of oysters to the gallon, eastern oysters are usually packed in the following grades:

Counts or Extra Large	*Not more than 160*
Extra Selects or Large	*161 to 210*
Selects or Medium	*211 to 300*
Standards or Small	*301 to 500*
Standards or Very Small	*Over 500*

ESCALLOPED OYSTERS I

Yield: 28 portions

Ingredients

CREAM SAUCE, MEDIUM	1 gallon
CRACKERS, SALTINES, crushed	1-1/2 quarts (1 pound)
OYSTERS (SELECTS)	2 quarts
BUTTER	1 pound
WHITE PEPPER	1 teaspoon
BREAD CRUMBS, buttered	2 cups
PAPRIKA	as needed

Procedure

1. Put 2 cups white sauce in bottom of each of four 10-inch by 12-inch pans. Scatter 1 cup broken crumbs over sauce, then layer 2 cups oysters on top. Dot with butter; sprinkle with pepper.
2. Scatter 1/2 cup cracker crumbs over top of oysters; spread 2 cups white sauce on top of crackers. Sprinkle with 1/2 cup buttered bread crumbs. Sprinkle with paprika.
3. Bake in oven at 350°F. for 35 minutes, or until crumbs are brown and oysters are done, but still soft and tender.

Oyster Bisque

Wheat Flour Institute

ESCALLOPED OYSTERS II

Yield: 48 portions

Ingredients

OYSTERS, drained	1 gallon
OYSTER LIQUOR	1 quart
CELERY, chopped	1 quart
BUTTER or MARGARINE	8 ounces
FLOUR	1-1/2 cups
SALT	2-1/2 tablespoons
PEPPER	1 teaspoon
MILK	3 quarts
BREAD CUBES, fresh	2 gallons (2-1/2 pounds)
BUTTER, melted	2 ounces
BREAD CRUMBS, dry	2 cups

Procedure

1. Drain oysters, reserving liquor.
2. Cook celery in oyster liquor 15 minutes.
3. Melt butter; blend in flour, salt, and pepper.
4. Gradually add milk; cook and stir until thick and smooth.
5. Add celery and oyster liquor.
6. Alternate layers of bread cubes, oysters, and celery cream sauce in 2 greased 12-inch by 20-inch by 2-1/2-inch pans with sauce as top layer.
7. Combine melted butter and dry crumbs, sprinkle over top of pans.
8. Bake in oven at 425°F. for 30 minutes.

OYSTERS JAMBALAYA

Yield: 100 portions

Ingredients

ONION, chopped	1-1/2 pounds
GARLIC	2 cloves
GREEN PEPPER, chopped	2 pounds
SHORTENING	2 pounds
FLOUR	1-1/2 pounds
OYSTER LIQUOR	2 gallons
TOMATOES, FRESH, peeled, diced	10 pounds
SALT	4 ounces
WHITE PEPPER	1 ounce
OYSTERS	24 pounds
HAM, cooked, chopped	5 pounds

Procedure

1. Saute onion, garlic, and green pepper in shortening. Add flour; blend; cook 5 minutes.
2. Add oyster liquor, tomatoes, and seasonings. Cook 10 minutes.
3. Add oysters and ham. Heat slowly until edges of oysters curl.
4. Serve in individual casseroles.

OYSTER FRICASSEE WITH RICE

Yield: 24 portions

Ingredients

OYSTERS	2 quarts
MILK	2 quarts
ONIONS, chopped	3 medium
MARGARINE or BUTTER	4 ounces
FLOUR	3/4 cup
SALT	2 teaspoons
CAYENNE PEPPER	1/4 teaspoon
EGGS, hard-cooked	24
RICE, cooked	1 gallon
PARSLEY, finely chopped	1/4 cup

Procedure

1. Heat oysters gently in their own liquor just until edges curl; remove from the liquor.
2. Combine the oyster liquor and milk; heat.
3. Saute onion in butter until transparent. Blend in flour.
4. Add the hot liquid; cook until thickened, stirring constantly. Add seasonings and oysters.
5. Shell eggs; cut in half.
6. Use 2 pans: arrange 2 quarts of rice in one half of each 12-inch by 20-inch pan; sprinkle with paprika.
7. Place 24 halves of eggs alongside the rice; pour 1/2 the hot oyster mixture over the eggs. Garnish with chopped parsley.

Crab Louis (above); Scallops Espanol *(Recipe on page 170)*

National Fisheries Institute

Scallops

SCALLOPS ALWAYS come to the market in the form of dressed meat. They are removed from the shells before the fishing vessels reach the shore.

Bay scallops are taken from inlets and bays. They are small, pinkish white, tender, and sweet. Distribution is mostly limited to the East Coast where they appear on the market as a fresh product.

Sea scallops are harvested from deep waters. Larger than bay scallops, they may be 1 or 2 in. across. Their color is creamy white. Sea scallops are available fresh; frozen; frozen breaded, ready-to-cook; and frozen, breaded, pre-cooked, ready for heating.

Firm, meaty, and definite in shape, scallops lend themselves to deep-frying, sauteing, broiling, and poaching. They appear to splendid advantage in casseroles and creamed dishes where more than one kind of seafood has a part.

PEPPER SCALLOPS →

Yield: 24 portions

Ingredients

SCALLOPS	12 dozen (approximately 6 pounds)
GREEN PEPPERS, cut into 1/2-inch squares	6
RED PEPPERS, cut into 1/2-inch squares	6
BUTTER or MARGARINE	1-1/2 pounds
SALT	as needed
WHITE WINE	1-1/2 cups
BREAD, toasted	24 slices

SCALLOPS ESPAGNOLE

(See picture, page 168)

Yield: 6 quarts, 36 2/3-cup portions

Ingredients

SCALLOPS, FRESH or FROZEN	5 pounds
ONION, chopped	2 cups
GREEN PEPPER, chopped	1 cup
BUTTER or MARGARINE	12 ounces
SALT	1-1/2 tablespoons
SUGAR	1/4 cup
CAYENNE PEPPER	1/2 teaspoon
MUSHROOMS, CANNED, sliced	1 cup
TOMATOES, CANNED, WITH JUICE	2 quarts
TAPIOCA, QUICK COOKING	1/4 cup

Procedure

1. Partially thaw frozen scallops, placing in colander to drain.
2. Saute onion and green pepper in butter until tender.
3. Add salt, sugar, cayenne, mushrooms, tomatoes, and tapioca.
4. Bring to boil. Reduce heat; simmer 15 minutes, stirring frequently.
5. Add scallops; simmer just until scallops are done, approximately 10 minutes.
6. Serve over rice.

Note

If thicker sauce is desired, adjust thickening with cornstarch blended with tomato juice or water.

Procedure

1. Saute scallops and pieces of green and red pepper in butter until tender.
2. Season; add wine.
3. Serve on toast.

SCALLOPS BROILED IN GARLIC BUTTER

Yield: 24 portions

Ingredients

SCALLOPS	8 pounds
GARLIC	6 cloves
BUTTER or MARGARINE	1 pound
CHIVES or SCALLIONS, chopped	1/4 cup
PARSLEY, chopped	6 tablespoons
TARRAGON, DRIED (optional)	1 teaspoon
SALT	1-1/2 teaspoons
BLACK PEPPER, freshly ground	1/2 teaspoon

Procedure

1. Wash scallops; drain on paper towels. Arrange on a shallow, flat pan.
2. Split garlic cloves; saute in butter until lightly browned. Discard garlic. Add chives or scallions, parsley, tarragon, salt, and pepper. Mix well; pour over the scallops. Marinate for 1/2 to 1 hour, or until ready to broil.
3. Broil under moderate heat, 3 minutes on each side, or until scallops are golden brown and bubbly. (Turn with a griddle turner.) Baste once or twice while broiling.

CREAMED SCALLOPS

Yield: 45 portions, approximately 6 ounces each

Ingredients

SEA SCALLOPS, FRESH or FROZEN	15 pounds
MUSHROOMS, FRESH, sliced	2 pounds
WATER	1-1/2 cups
BUTTER or MARGARINE	3/4 pound
FLOUR	1-1/2 cups (6 ounces)
SALT	1-1/2 tablespoons
PEPPER	1 teaspoon
MILK, WHOLE	2 quarts
EVAPORATED MILK	3 14-1/2-ounce cans
PARSLEY, minced	1/4 cup
CHEESE, AMERICAN, grated	1 pound

Procedure

1. If scallops are frozen, defrost. Rinse and dry. Spread half of scallops in each of two 12-inch by 18-inch by 2-inch baking pans.
2. Cook mushrooms in water for 5 minutes. Drain.
3. Melt butter; blend in flour, salt, and pepper. Cook over low heat about 5 minutes.
4. Add milk and evaporated milk. Cook and stir until smooth and thickened. Add parsley and mushrooms.
5. Divide sauce between the two baking pans, stirring into scallops.
6. Sprinkle cheese over top of each pan. Bake in oven at 325°F. for 35 to 40 minutes. Serve on toast points. Garnish with pimiento or parsley if desired.

CHINESE STYLE SCALLOPS

Yield: 50 portions

Ingredients

LEMON JUICE	1/4 cup
WATER, cold	1 gallon
SCALLOPS, LARGE	3 quarts
WATER, boiling	1 gallon
SALT	1 tablespoon
MUSHROOMS	3 pounds
SALT	1 tablespoon
SHORTENING	12 ounces
CORNSTARCH	8 ounces
WATER, cold	1 cup
CARAMEL COLOR	1 tablespoon
SOY SAUCE	1 cup
RICE, cooked	2 gallons

Procedure

1. Add lemon juice to cold water. Wash scallops; drain.
2. Cut scallops into quarters; add to boiling water. Add first amount of salt; cook until scallops are just tender, 2 to 3 minutes. Drain, reserving liquid.
3. Slice mushrooms; season with remaining salt. Saute in shortening until tender. Drain, reserving liquid.
4. Combine drained liquid from scallops and from mushrooms. Blend cornstarch with remaining cold water; add to liquid. Cook and stir until clear. Add caramel color and soy sauce.
5. Add scallops and mushrooms to the sauce; heat. Let stand over hot water to allow flavors to blend. Serve over hot rice.

Lemon Clam Spaghetti

Durum Macaroni HRI Program

Clams

CLAMS PROVIDE the inspiration for attractive appetizers, entrees, and soups. In addition, they can, now and then, provide an interesting alternate in dishes that call for oysters or mussels.

Fresh, raw clams come to the market both in the shell and shucked. The shucked clams (removed from the shell) are also available canned, either whole or minced. Clam juice can be either a canned or bottled item. Frozen clams and frozen, breaded, fried clams are other market forms.

Clams from the Atlantic coast are classified as hard-shell or soft-shell. The hard-shell variety is nearly round in shape, and is obtained by raking or dredging from waters a few fathoms deep. These clams are often referred to as "quahogs," a holdover from Indian times.

The smaller quahogs, known as littlenecks and cherrystones, are widely acclaimed for on-the-half-shell service, either raw or cooked. It is not as well known, but these small hard-shell clams make a very special treat when steamed. Larger hard-shell clams are good for chowder use.

Soft-shell clams inhabit the waters closer to shore and are dug from the sand or mud. They are more oval than round in shape. Another characteristic is a rather long, ungainly neck. Soft-shell clams are so frequently used for steaming that they have earned the name of "steamers." They also make a popular fried specialty and an appealing broth. And, they are the proper clams to use when staging an authentic New England clam bake.

The varieties of clams harvested from the Pacific include the razor, butter, pismo, and geoduck. In addition, the soft- and hard-shell clams described above, which are of Atlantic origin, have been successfully transplanted to the Pacific coast.

CROW'S NEST CLAM SCALLOP

Yield: 25 portions

Ingredients	
CLAMS, ground	2 quarts
CRACKERS, SODA, crushed	2 cups
CLAM NECTAR or CANNED CLAM BROTH	1 cup
EGGS, well beaten	6
BUTTER or MARGARINE, melted	1/4 cup
MILK	1 quart
CELERY, ground	1-1/2 cups
ONION, ground	1/2 cup
SALT	as needed
PEPPER	as needed

Procedure

1. Combine ingredients; toss together until well mixed. Turn into a 12-inch by 20-inch by 2-1/4-inch baking pan.
2. Bake in oven at 350°F. for 50 minutes. Serve garnished with sliced spanish olives and parsley sprigs, if desired.

Nooner II

National Sandwich Idea Headquarters

MEDIA DOLMA
(Stuffed Clams, Armenian Style)

Yield: 24 portions

Ingredients

*CLAMS, shucked	1 gallon
ONION, finely chopped	1 quart
OLIVE OIL	3/4 cup
SALT	1 teaspoon
ALLSPICE, GROUND	1-1/2 teaspoons
BLACK PEPPER	1 teaspoon
RICE, UNCOOKED	2 cups
CLAM LIQUOR	1-1/4 quarts
BUTTER or MARGARINE	6 ounces
CURRANTS, DRIED	1 cup
PARSLEY, chopped	1 cup
PINE NUTS, lightly toasted	1 cup

Procedure

1. Drain clams, reserving liquor. Chop clams.
2. Saute onion in olive oil until limp. Add seasonings and rice. Add clam liquor; bring to a boil. Cover; simmer 20 minutes or until rice is tender. Adjust seasoning, if necessary.
3. Heat butter slowly until brown. Add to cooked rice mixture together with clams, currants, parsley, and pine nuts. Toss gently to mix.
4. Spoon mixture into individual shell-shaped casseroles. Bake in oven at 350°F. until thoroughly heated.

*If desired, substitute live clams and spoon mixture into the shells.

Shrimp Romano

Shrimp Association of the Americas

Crisp-Coated Fried Shrimp

Kellogg Company

Shrimp

SHRIMP IN THE raw state are often called "green shrimp." Almost all of the shrimp sold today have the heads removed before they come to market. Thus the term "shrimp" commonly refers to the jointed rear or tail section, the part with the meat.

Shrimp sizes or grades are based on the number of shrimp to the pound. They range from Extra Colossal (under 10 to the pound) to Tiny (over 70 to the pound.) Large shrimp, midway in the range, run 31 to 35 to the pound. Purchase prices tend to be higher on the larger sizes, but there is the advantage that they take less time to shell and devein. Large or small, shrimp are equally tasty and find a warm welcome as a menu item.

They are on the market in a variety of forms:

1. *Fresh or frozen, in the shell or peeled*
2. *Fresh or frozen, peeled and deveined*
3. *Fresh or frozen, cooked, peeled, and deveined*
4. *Frozen, raw, breaded, ready for cooking*
5. *Frozen, breaded, cooked, ready for heating*
6. *Canned, packed in natural juices or dry*

CHINESE SHRIMP WITH PEA PODS
(Cooked-to-Order)

Yield: 2 portions

Ingredients	
CHINESE PEA PODS, FROZEN, thawed	1/2 cup
GINGER ROOT, FRESH, grated	1/2 teaspoon
SHERRY, DRY	1 teaspoon
CORNSTARCH	1 teaspoon
SALT	1/8 teaspoon
SCALLION, cut in 2-inch pieces	1 small
SHRIMP, RAW, shelled, deveined	10-1/2 ounces
COOKING OIL	1/2 cup
CORNSTARCH	1/2 teaspoon
WATER, cold	1 tablespoon
COOKING OIL	1-1/2 tablespoons
WATER CHESTNUTS, drained, sliced	1/2 cup

Procedure

1. Thaw frozen pea pods by placing in hot water; drain and measure required amount.
2. Combine ginger root, sherry, first amount of cornstarch, salt, scallion, and shrimp.
3. Heat first amount of oil in skillet over high heat. Add shrimp mixture; turn constantly until shrimp turn pink, about 1 to 2 minutes.
4. Drain shrimp. Discard scallion. Wipe out skillet.
5. Blend cornstarch with cold water.
6. Add second amount of oil to clean skillet over medium heat. Add pea pods; stir until thoroughly heated, about 1 minute.
7. Add water chestnuts and blended cornstarch, continuing to stir until mixture thickens.
8. Add cooked shrimp; heat through and serve.

SHRIMP LOUISIANE

Yield: 48 portions

Ingredients

WATER	1-1/2 gallons
VINEGAR	1 cup
ONION FLAKES	1/2 cup
CELERY FLAKES	1/4 cup
PARSLEY FLAKES	1/4 cup
BAY LEAVES	4
SALT	3 tablespoons
PEPPERCORNS, WHOLE	2 tablespoons
THYME LEAVES	1 tablespoon
SHRIMP (16 to 20 COUNT)	16 pounds
BUTTER or MARGARINE	1 pound
FLOUR	8 ounces
PAPRIKA	1/2 cup
SALT	3 tablespoons
WHITE PEPPER	1 teaspoon
COOKING LIQUID from shrimp	1 gallon
TOMATO SAUCE	2 cups
CREAM, LIGHT	1 quart
RICE, cooked, hot	2 gallons

Procedure

1. Combine water, vinegar, onion flakes, celery flakes, parsley flakes, bay leaves, first amount of salt, peppercorns, and thyme. Bring to boiling point.
2. Add shrimp; return to boil. Reduce heat; cook 5 minutes.
3. Let shrimp cool slightly in liquid for 15 minutes. Strain, reserving liquid.
4. Shell and devein shrimp. Cut into pieces.
5. Melt butter; blend in flour, paprika, salt, and white pepper. Cook 2 minutes.
6. Gradually add required amount of reserved cooking liquid. Cook and stir until smooth. Add tomato sauce; cook over low heat 25 to 30 minutes.
7. Add cream and cooked shrimp. Heat through, *do not boil.*
8. Serve with rice.

SHRIMP IN SKILLET

→

Yield: 30 4-ounce portions

Ingredients	
SHRIMP, RAW, in SHELL	15 pounds
BUTTER or MARGARINE	1 pound
GARLIC, minced	4 cloves
SALT	2 tablespoons
MONOSODIUM GLUTAMATE	2 tablespoons
PEPPER	1/4 teaspoon
PARSLEY, finely chopped	1 cup

SHRIMP PIE

Yield: 30 portions

Ingredients	
SHRIMP, FROZEN, shelled, cleaned	8 pounds
WHITE SAUCE or CREAM of CELERY SOUP, CONDENSED	2 quarts
CHEESE, CHEDDAR, grated	1 pound
CELERY, chopped	1-1/2 quarts
GREEN PEPPER, chopped	2 cups
ONION, finely chopped	2 cups
PIE PASTRY	as needed

Procedure

1. Cook shrimp; drain. Cool. Set aside 30 shrimp for garnish.
2. Combine white sauce and cheese; heat and stir until cheese is melted. Add celery, green pepper, and onion.
3. Roll out pastry. Cut into 7-inch squares. Place each square in an aluminum foil pan or other individual pie pan.
4. Divide shrimp evenly in pans. Pour a scant 2/3 cup of the sauce over the shrimp in each pan. Fold up the pastry so the corners meet in the center. Seal edges together except at the center. Turn the points back; insert one of the reserved shrimp in the opening as a garnish.
5. Bake in oven at 400°F. for 25 minutes or until golden brown.

Procedure

1. Shell, devein, and wash the raw shrimp. Drain well.
2. Melt butter; add garlic and seasonings. Cook until garlic is lightly browned. Remove garlic pieces.
3. Add shrimp; cook until shrimp turns pink and is just done, turning only once. Sprinkle with parsley; continue cooking for only one minute more. Serve piping hot.

Note

This may be prepared in quantity for group feeding, or cooked to order and served in individual skillet.

ROSY SHRIMP STROGANOFF

Yield: 32 6-ounce portions with 6 ounces noodles

Ingredients

BUTTER or MARGARINE	12 ounces
FLOUR	6 ounces
TOMATO JUICE	2 quarts
ONION, grated	1/2 cup
PREPARED MUSTARD	2 tablespoons
SHRIMP, RAW, shelled, deveined	4 pounds
SOUR CREAM	3 cups
SALT	as needed
PEPPER	as needed
NOODLES, cooked, hot	1-1/2 gallons
PARSLEY, chopped	as needed

Procedure

1. Melt butter; blend in flour. Gradually add tomato juice, onion, and mustard; cook and stir until sauce bubbles and thickens.
2. Add shrimp; simmer just until shrimp are firm.
3. Blend in sour cream. Heat, but do not boil. Season with salt and pepper.
4. Garnish hot noodles with parsley. Serve shrimp over noodles.

CELERY AND SHRIMP HAWAIIAN

Yield: 48 portions

Ingredients

CELERY, cut diagonally into 1/2-inch slices	2 gallons
BEEF BROTH	1-1/2 gallons
SHRIMP, RAW, shelled, deveined	10 pounds
CHINESE PEA PODS, FROZEN, thawed	6 pounds
WATER CHESTNUTS, drained, sliced	2 1-pound cans
SOY SAUCE	3/4 cup
TARRAGON LEAVES, CRUMBLED	1 tablespoon
SALT	1 tablespoon
GINGER, GROUND	1 tablespoon
WHITE PEPPER	1 teaspoon
MUSHROOMS, SLICED	3 1-pound cans
LIQUID from MUSHROOMS	1 quart
CORNSTARCH	1-1/2 cups
RICE, cooked, hot	2 gallons

Procedure

1. Combine celery and broth. Heat to boiling point. Cook, uncovered, 8 minutes.
2. Add shrimp, pea pods, water chestnuts, soy sauce, tarragon, salt, ginger, and white pepper. Cook, stirring occasionally, 10 minutes or until celery and shrimp are tender.
3. Drain mushrooms, reserving required amount of liquid. Add mushrooms to shrimp mixture.
4. Blend cornstarch and mushroom liquid; stir into hot mixture. Cook until thickened.
5. Serve over rice.

GREEN BEANS AND SHRIMP POLYNESIAN

Yield: 5-1/2 quarts, 24 portions

Ingredients

PINEAPPLES, FRESH, SMALL*	12
FRUIT from PINEAPPLES, diced	1-1/4 quarts
SHRIMP, RAW, MEDIUM SIZE, shelled, deveined	3 pounds
BROWN SUGAR	1-1/2 cups (9 ounces)
CORNSTARCH	3/4 cup
JUICE from PINEAPPLES and/or WATER	3 cups
VINEGAR	1-1/2 cups
SOY SAUCE	6 tablespoons
SALT	1 tablespoon
GREEN BEANS, DIAGONAL CUT, drained	1 No. 10 can
MARASCHINO CHERRIES, drained, halved	1-1/2 cups
WATER CHESTNUTS, drained, sliced	2 8-1/2-ounce cans

*If desired, substitute two 1-pound, 4-ounce cans (5 cups) of pineapple tidbits, drained, for the fresh pineapple. Serve mixture over hot cooked rice.

Procedure

1. Halve pineapples lengthwise, cutting through leaves and keeping them intact. Loosen fruit from shell, being careful not to puncture shell.
2. Scoop out fruit from shells; core and dice to make required amount. Reserve juice. (Save remaining pineapple for other use.)
3. Cook shrimp according to package directions; drain.
4. Combine brown sugar and cornstarch; add pineapple juice and/or water, vinegar, soy sauce, and salt. Cook and stir until thickened and bubbly.
5. Add diced pineapple, shrimp, beans, cherries, and water chestnuts. Heat through, stirring occasionally.
6. Heat pineapple shells in oven at 350°F. for 10 minutes.
7. Spoon hot mixture into shells.

SWEET AND SOUR SHRIMP
(Cooked-to-Order)

Yield: 2 portions

Ingredients	
SHERRY, DRY	1 teaspoon
SOY SAUCE	1 teaspoon
CORNSTARCH	1 tablespoon
SALT	1/8 teaspoon
SHRIMP, RAW, shelled, deveined	10-1/2 ounces
COOKING OIL	1/2 cup
CORNSTARCH	2 teaspoons
WATER, cold	2 tablespoons
COOKING OIL	1 tablespoon
GREEN PEPPER, cut in strips	1
PINEAPPLE JUICE	1/3 cup
VINEGAR	1/4 cup
BROWN SUGAR, packed	1/3 cup
PINEAPPLE CUBES, drained	1/2 cup
PIMIENTO, diced	1/2 teaspoon

Procedure

1. Combine sherry, soy sauce, first amount of cornstarch, salt, and shrimp.
2. Heat first amount of oil in skillet over high heat. Add shrimp mixture; turn constantly until shrimp turn pink, about 1 to 2 minutes. Drain shrimp; set aside. Wipe out skillet.
3. Blend remaining cornstarch with water.
4. Add second amount of oil to clean skillet over medium heat. Add green pepper strips; stir until thoroughly heated, about 1 minute.
5. Stir in pineapple juice, vinegar, soy sauce, and brown sugar. Add blended cornstarch; stir constantly until mixture thickens.
6. Add pineapple, pimiento, and shrimp. Mix gently; heat through and serve.

Sunny Seas Rarebit
Cling Peach Advisory Board

SHRIMP PILAF

Yield: 50 portions

Ingredients

RICE, UNCOOKED	2 quarts
BUTTER or MARGARINE	12 ounces
ONIONS, chopped	8 medium
GREEN PEPPER, diced	1-1/2 quarts
CELERY, diced	2-1/2 quarts
TOMATO JUICE	1-1/2 gallons
BEEF BOUILLON	2-1/2 quarts
PARSLEY, minced	1-1/2 cups
CAYENNE PEPPER	2 teaspoons
SUMMER SAVORY	2 teaspoons
SALT	4 teaspoons
SHRIMP, cooked, shelled, deveined	8 pounds
GUMBO FILE	1 teaspoon

Procedure

1. Saute rice in butter, stirring frequently, until golden brown.
2. Stir in onion, green pepper, celery, tomato juice, and bouillon. Cover tightly; bake in oven at 375°F. for 30 minutes.
3. Stir lightly with fork. Add parsley, cayenne, summer savory, salt, and shrimp.
4. Return to oven; cook 20 minutes. Stir in gumbo file.

SHRIMP CREOLE I →

Yield: 48 portions

Ingredients	
SHRIMP, FRESH or FROZEN	15 pounds
ONION, chopped	1 quart
GARLIC, minced	1 clove
GREEN PEPPER, chopped	1 quart
BUTTER or COOKING OIL	1 cup
FLOUR	5 ounces
SALT	3 tablespoons
PEPPER	2 teaspoons
TOMATOES, CANNED	1-1/4 gallons
RICE, cooked	1-1/2 gallons

SHRIMP CREOLE II

Yield: 50 portions

Ingredients	
ONION, chopped	1 pound
BUTTER or MARGARINE	6 ounces
GARLIC, minced	1 clove
PEPPER	1 tablespoon
SALT	6 tablespoons
TOMATOES, CANNED	1-1/2 quarts
STOCK	1-1/2 quarts
PIMIENTO, diced	12 ounces
GREEN PEPPER, chopped	8 ounces
SHRIMP, cooked	5 pounds
CLOVES, WHOLE	3
CORNSTARCH	3/4 cup
RICE, cooked	1-1/4 gallons

Procedure

1. Brown onions in butter. Add garlic and saute.
2. Add remaining ingredients except rice. Simmer 30 minutes.
3. Serve 6 ounces Shrimp Creole over No. 16 scoop rice.

Procedure

1. Cook shrimp. Shell; devein.
2. Saute onion, garlic, and green pepper in butter until tender but not brown. Blend in flour and seasonings.
3. Add tomatoes; cook and stir until thickened. Add shrimp; heat.
4. Serve 3/4 cup Shrimp Creole over 1/2 cup rice.

SHRIMP-CROWNED CURRIED RICE

Yield: 2 gallons, 32 1-cup portions

Ingredients

ONION, thinly sliced	1-1/2 pounds
BUTTER	3/4 pound
APPLESAUCE	1 No. 10 can
RICE, cooked	3 quarts
RAISINS	1 pound
SALT	1 tablespoon
CURRY POWDER	2 tablespoons
OREGANO, LEAF, crumbled	1 tablespoon
SHRIMP, cooked	4 pounds
BUTTER, melted	6 ounces

Procedure

1. Saute onion in butter until lightly browned and soft in texture.
2. Add applesauce, rice, raisins, salt, curry powder, and oregano. Place in baking pans.
3. Arrange shrimp over the top of rice and applesauce mixture. Brush with melted butter. Cover pan with foil; bake in oven at 350°F. for 45 minutes.

BENGAL SHRIMP CURRY

Yield: 48 portions

Ingredients

SHRIMP, RAW, cleaned	12 pounds
BUTTER	3/4 pound
INSTANT MINCED ONION	1/3 cup
FLOUR	1-1/2 cups
CURRY POWDER	1/2 cup
GARLIC POWDER	1/2 teaspoon
CELERY FLAKES	2 tablespoons
APPLES, finely diced	2 cups
COCONUT, grated	1/4 cup
LEMON JUICE	2 tablespoons
SALT	1 teaspoon
WHITE PEPPER	1/2 teaspoon
GINGER, GROUND	1/4 teaspoon
CHUTNEY (optional)	1/2 cup
CASHEW NUTS, chopped	1/2 cup
STOCK, hot	1 gallon
CREAM, hot	2 cups
RICE, cooked, hot	5 pounds

Procedure

1. Dice shrimp. Melt butter in a heavy 5-gallon pot. Add shrimp; saute lightly. Add onion, flour, curry powder, garlic powder, celery flakes, apples, and coconut. Blend; cook over low heat 5 minutes.

2. Add lemon juice, salt, pepper, ginger, chutney, cashew nuts, and hot stock, stirring continuously until smooth. Bring to a boil; cook over low heat for 30 minutes.

3. Stir in hot cream. Correct seasoning, if necessary. Serve over hot rice.

FIESTA SHRIMP POT

Yield: 24 portions

Ingredients

SHRIMP, FROZEN	4-1/2 pounds
OKRA, FROZEN	20 ounces
RICE, UNCOOKED	1 quart
ONION, FROZEN, CHOPPED	1 cup
GREEN PEPPER, FROZEN, CHOPPED	1 cup
GARLIC, minced	3 cloves
OLIVE OIL	1 cup
WATER	2 quarts
TOMATO SAUCE	2 cups
LEMON JUICE	2/3 cup
SALT	1 tablespoon
PEPPER	1/2 teaspoon
OREGANO	1-1/2 teaspoons
SUCCOTASH, FROZEN	20 ounces
GREEN BEANS, FROZEN, CUT	9 ounces

Procedure

1. Cook shrimp. Shell, devein. Keep warm.
2. Partially thaw okra, if necessary to separate pieces.
3. Add rice, onion, green pepper, and garlic to olive oil. Heat and stir until rice is lightly browned.
4. Add water, tomato sauce, lemon juice, seasonings, succotash, and green beans. Heat until vegetables are thawed and mixture comes to a boil.
5. Stir. Cover; cook over low heat 25 minutes.
6. Add okra; cook 15 minutes longer or until rice and vegetables are done.
7. Turn into steam table pan or individual serving dishes. Arrange warm shrimp on top.

BARBECUED BUTTERFLY SHRIMP →

Yield: 24 portions

Ingredients

SOY SAUCE	2/3 cup
HONEY	1/4 cup
SHERRY	1/4 cup
WATER	2/3 cup
GARLIC, minced	1 clove
GINGER ROOT, FRESH, grated	1-1/2 teaspoons
BUTTERFLY SHRIMP, FROZEN, LARGE, BREADED	8 pounds

SPECIALTY-OF-THE-HOUSE SHRIMP

Yield: 24 4-ounce portions (6 shrimp and sauce)

Ingredients

SHRIMP, MEDIUM, RAW	6 pounds
WHITE WINE, DRY	2 cups
SALAD OIL	2 cups
GREEN ONIONS, finely sliced	14 to 16
PARSLEY, chopped	1/4 cup
THYME, DILL, or TARRAGON	pinch
PEPPER	1/2 teaspoon
SALT	2 teaspoons
MONOSODIUM GLUTAMATE	1 teaspoon

Procedure

1. Remove shell from shrimp, taking off all but last segment and tail. Devein.
2. Combine wine, oil, green onions, parsley, and seasonings. Add shrimp; let stand several hours or overnight to marinate.
3. Arrange shrimp in rows on sheetpans. Pour any remaining marinade over shrimp.
4. Place in very hot broiler for 1 minute or until all shrimp turn bright pink. Turn and broil 1 to 2 minutes on other side. Serve moistened with marinade from pans.

Procedure

1. Combine soy sauce, honey, sherry, water, garlic, and ginger root in saucepan. Blend thoroughly over medium heat until heated through.

2. Fry shrimp in deep fat according to label directions. Serve with hot barbecue sauce.

SHRIMP CREOLE VIOLA

Yield: 80 portions

Ingredients

TOMATOES	2 No. 10 cans
TOMATO PUREE	1 No. 10 can
CHICKEN STOCK	1 gallon
GREEN ONIONS, chopped	1 quart
GREEN PEPPER, chopped	1 quart
CELERY, chopped	1 quart
MUSHROOMS, BUTTON	2 quarts
SALT	3 tablespoons
SUGAR	1/4 cup
OREGANO	2 tablespoons
PAPRIKA	1/4 cup
LIQUID HOT PEPPER SEASONING	1 teaspoon
BAY LEAVES	2
SHRIMP, FRESH, shelled, deveined	20 pounds
RICE, cooked, hot	3-1/4 gallons

Procedure

1. Combine tomatoes, tomato puree, chicken stock, vegetables, and seasonings. Simmer 2 hours.

2. Add raw shrimp to sauce; simmer only until shrimp are done. Do not overcook.

3. Serve over steamed rice.

POACHED EGGS, SEAFOOD ROYAL

Yield: 16 portions

Ingredients

BAKING POTATOES	16
MILK, hot	1 cup (about)
SALT and PEPPER	as needed
ONION, finely chopped	1/2 cup
BUTTER or MARGARINE	1/4 pound
FLOUR	1/2 cup
SALT	1 teaspoon
PEPPER	1/4 teaspoon
PAPRIKA	1/4 teaspoon
MILK	2 cups
CHICKEN BROTH	2 cups
WORCESTERSHIRE SAUCE	1 teaspoon
EGG YOLKS, beaten	3
SHRIMP (cooked weight)	14 ounces
EGGS, poached	32

Procedure

1. Bake potatoes. Cut a slice from the top of each; scoop out insides. Mash potatoes adding hot milk and salt and pepper to season.

2. Place a layer of the mashed potato in the bottom of each potato shell.

3. Cook onion in butter until tender but not brown; blend in flour, salt, pepper, and paprika.

4. Add milk, broth, and Worcestershire sauce all at once. Cook and stir until thickened and smooth. Remove from heat; add egg yolks; blend well. Add shrimp.

5. Fill potato shells with shrimp sauce. Bake in oven at 400°F. for 5 to 10 minutes or until potatoes are heated through. Top with poached eggs.

SHRIMP-RICE CASSEROLE WITH SHERRY SAUCE

Yield: 48 portions

Ingredients	
ONION, finely chopped	1-1/2 cups
BUTTER or MARGARINE	1-1/2 pounds
FLOUR	2-1/2 cups
NONFAT DRY MILK	1-1/2 pounds
WATER, warm	1-1/2 gallons
SALT	2 tablespoons
WHITE PEPPER	1 teaspoon
LIQUID HOT PEPPER SEASONING	few drops
NUTMEG	as needed
SHERRY	1-1/2 to 2 cups
RICE, cooked (unsalted)	1-1/2 gallons
SHRIMP, cooked	6 pounds
PAPRIKA	as needed

Procedure

1. Saute onion in butter until clear. Remove from heat.
2. Sift flour and nonfat dry milk together. Blend with the butter and onion.
3. Add warm water, mixing until smooth. Bring sauce slowly to a rolling boil, stirring constantly. Remove from heat. Add salt, pepper, hot pepper seasoning, and nutmeg. Keep sauce hot over hot water. Add sherry just before using.
4. To serve: place 1/2 cup rice in casserole. Top with 2 ounces shrimp. Pour 5 ounces of sauce over each casserole; sprinkle with paprika.
5. Place casseroles under broiler, about 3 inches from heat, until bubbly and lightly browned.

SHRIMP SARAPICIO →

Yield: 1 portion

Ingredients

CHEESE, CREAM	2 ounces
CHEESE, ROQUEFORT	2 ounces
FRENCH TRUFFLE, chopped (optional)	1
PIMIENTO, chopped	1
SHRIMP, RAW, cleaned	6 ounces
LEMON SLICES	2
CHAMPAGNE, SAUTERNE, or ROSE WINE	1 ounce

PINEAPPLE SHRIMP TOSS

Yield: 32 portions

Ingredients

FLOUR	1 cup
GARLIC SALT	4 teaspoons
SHRIMP, LARGE, cooked	4 pounds
BUTTER or MARGARINE	1/2 pound
CELERY, cut in 1-inch diagonal slices	1 gallon
PINEAPPLE CHUNKS	1 No. 10 can
PINEAPPLE SYRUP and WATER to equal	5-1/3 cups
VINEGAR	1 cup
SOY SAUCE	1 cup
CORNSTARCH	1/2 cup
STOCK	2 cups
GREEN ONIONS, cut in 3- to 4-inch lengths	2 quarts

Procedure

1. Mix flour and garlic salt.
2. Toss shrimp in seasoned flour. Cook in butter over moderate heat until lightly browned.
3. Add celery. Cover; cook 5 minutes.
4. Drain pineapple. Add water to syrup to make required amount.
5. Add syrup, vinegar, and soy sauce to shrimp mixture.
6. Blend cornstarch and stock. Add to shrimp mixture; cook, stirring, until sauce boils.
7. Add onions and pineapple chunks. Heat five minutes longer.

Procedure

1. Mix cheeses, truffle, and pimiento into a paste. Spread on a square of aluminum foil.
2. Place shrimp on paste; put lemon slices on top. Pour champagne over shrimp.
3. Fold foil, closing into a packet. Bake in oven at 400°F. for 20 to 30 minutes. Open foil; pour shrimp into a patty shell.

SAVORY SHRIMP AND RICE

Yield: 50 portions

Ingredients

PARSLEY, chopped	1 cup
PIMIENTO, finely chopped	1 cup
ONION, grated	1/2 cup
SALT	2 teaspoons
WHITE PEPPER	2 teaspoons
BUTTER or MARGARINE, melted	1 pound
RICE, cooked, hot	1-1/2 gallons
SHRIMP, RAW, cleaned	12 pounds
MUSHROOM SOUP, CANNED	5 pounds, 4 ounces
CREAM	1-1/4 quarts
CHICKEN STOCK	1 cup
LEMON JUICE	1/2 cup
BAY LEAF	1 small
PAPRIKA	2 teaspoons

Procedure

1. Add parsley, pimiento, onion, salt, 1 teaspoon of the pepper, and 1 cup (1/2 pound) of the butter to the hot rice; toss lightly.
2. Cook cleaned shrimp slowly in remaining butter until lightly browned. Add soup, cream, chicken stock, lemon juice, bay leaf, and remaining pepper. Simmer until thoroughly heated. Remove bay leaf.
3. Serve shrimp over rice. Garnish with paprika.

Snails

SNAILS ARE ESTEEMED as a delicacy especially in Italy and France. They are becoming better known in this country as a novel and special treat. They are usually presented in their shells in grooved snail dishes with special forks and pincers for holding the shells while the contents are removed. Gourmets make something of a ritual of using these accessories and enjoying the snails.

Fresh, live-in-the-shell snails are available in some markets. Canned snails and snail shells (which come as a separate item) are more generally available.

Stuffed snails are prepared with a well-seasoned butter. A small lump of butter goes into the shell first, is then followed by the snail with more butter as the finishing touch. As the stuffed snails heat, the snails in the shell become bathed in butter sauce.

To present snails as an appetizer without the fanfare of shells, arrange snails in broiled or sauteed mushroom caps; put a dab of seasoned butter on top of each and broil until the butter is melted and the tidbits are hot.

Mussels

MUSSELS ARE not as well promoted as other shellfish, yet they can offer many exciting possibilities. They have an added special advantage of being available the year around.

Mussels are sold alive in their shells. Out-of-shell mussels are available canned. The flesh is yellow in color; the flavor, delicate and sweet. While mussels are edible raw, they are at their best when cooked.

Mussels can be steamed, stuffed, or used in creamed dishes, and in seafood casseroles, chowders, and bisques.

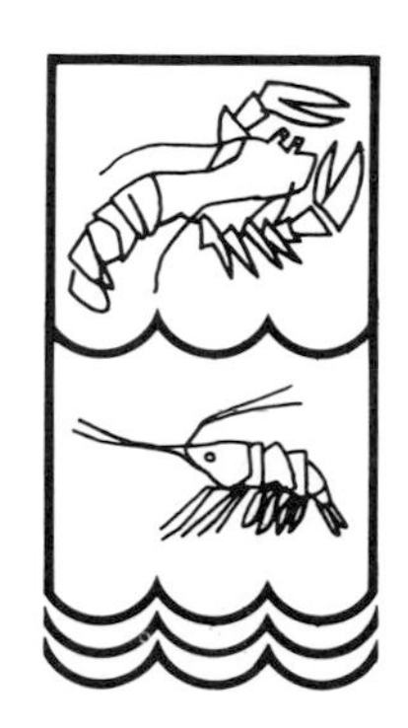

Seafood Medleys

Scandinavian Fish Pudding with Shrimp Sauce
(See recipe, page 114.)

National Fisheries Institute

DEEP SEA CASSEROLE

Yield: 32 portions

Ingredients

MACARONI SHELLS	2 pounds
CREAM of CELERY SOUP, CONDENSED	1 quart
CREAM of MUSHROOM SOUP, CONDENSED	2-1/2 cups
WATER	2 cups
LEMON JUICE	1/4 cup
CHEESE, CHEDDAR, grated	1 pound
SOY SAUCE	1-1/2 tablespoons
CRABMEAT	6 6-1/2-ounce cans
SHRIMP, cooked, shelled, deveined	2 pounds (ready-to-use weight)

Procedure

1. Cook macaroni shells according to package directions; drain.
2. Combine soups and water; heat. Add lemon juice, cheese, and soy sauce; stir until cheese is melted.
3. Drain crabmeat; remove any shell and cartilage. Flake, reserving some of the lumps for garnish.
4. Add remaining crabmeat and shrimp to soup mixture; heat.
5. Reserve some of the macaroni shells to use as a border for the tops of the casseroles. Fold remainder of the shells into the seafood mixture, continuing to heat.
6. Fill individual casseroles or baking pans. Top with reserved chunks of crabmeat; border with reserved shells.
7. Bake in oven at 375°F. for 15 minutes or until bubbly. Garnish with parsley, if desired.

Four Specialties from the Sea
(From top to bottom, Seagoing Spaghetti, Shrimp Quiche, Fish 'N Shells, Paella)

National Fisheries Institute

COQUILLE ALMONDINE

Yield: approximately 60 portions

Ingredients

ALMONDS, UNBLANCHED, SLICED	1-1/2 pounds
CREAM OF MUSHROOM SOUP, CONDENSED	2 50-ounce cans
EGG YOLKS	1-2/3 cups
CREAM, LIGHT	2-1/2 cups
VERMOUTH, DRY	2-1/2 cups
GARLIC POWDER	2-1/2 teaspoons
PIMIENTO, diced	1-1/4 cups
SCALLOPS, cut in 1/2-inch cubes	2-1/2 pounds
SOLE, cut in 3/4-inch squares	2-1/2 pounds
SHRIMP, SMALL, shelled	2-1/2 pounds
PEAS, FROZEN	1-1/4 quarts
YELLOW FOOD COLOR	as needed
BUTTER or MARGARINE	1 pound
BREAD CRUMBS, fine, dry	1-1/4 quarts
BASIL, CRUMBLED	2-1/2 teaspoons
OREGANO, CRUMBLED	2-1/2 teaspoons
SCALLOP SHELLS, 6-INCH, POLISHED	60

Procedure

1. Spread almonds in a shallow pan. Place in oven at 350°F. for 5 minutes or until light golden, stirring several times for even toasting. Divide toasted almonds into two equal amounts.
2. Combine soup, egg yolks, cream, vermouth, and garlic powder in kettle; mix, using a wire whip.
3. Add pimiento, half of the almonds, the scallops, sole, shrimp, and peas. Add yellow food color to tint a rich cream color. Heat to boiling, stirring often. Reduce heat; simmer 5 minutes.
4. Melt butter in a saucepot. Stir in crumbs, basil, and oregano.
5. Portion seafood mixture into warm scallop shells, allowing a generous 1/2 cup per shell. Sprinkle a border of crumbs around edge of filled shells. Sprinkle remaining toasted almonds across center of each.

Note

To prepare ahead of time, wrap each filled shell in foil, using a drugstore fold. Freeze or refrigerate. To reheat for serving, place wrapped shells in oven at 400°F. Allow 20 to 25 minutes for refrigerated shells; 30 to 35 minutes for frozen shells.

AVOCADO-SEAFOOD COQUILLE

Yield: 3-3/4 quarts, 22 2/3-cup portions

Ingredients

BUTTER or MARGARINE	1/2 pound
FLOUR	1 cup
SALT	1 tablespoon
PEPPER	1/2 teaspoon
MARJORAM, CRUSHED	2 teaspoons
CREAM, LIGHT	2 quarts
BUTTER or MARGARINE	1/4 pound
SCALLOPS, halved or quartered	3 pounds
SHRIMP, RAW, shelled, deveined	1 pound
SHERRY	1/2 cup
PARSLEY, chopped	1/4 cup
MUSHROOMS, CANNED, SLICED, drained	2 cups
AVOCADOS	8 to 9
LEMON JUICE	as needed
TARRAGON TOAST TRIANGLES*	88

Procedure

1. Melt first amount of butter in top of double boiler. Blend in flour, salt, pepper, and marjoram. Heat thoroughly.
2. Stir in cream, cook and stir until smooth and thickened. Keep warm.
3. Melt remaining butter in skillet. Add scallops and shrimp; saute, stirring occasionally, until seafood is done, about 4 to 5 minutes.
4. Add sherry, parsley, mushrooms, and seafood to cream sauce.
5. Cut avocados lengthwise into halves; remove seeds and skin. Cut each half into 4 slices; sprinkle with lemon juice.
6. To serve: place 2 tarragon toast triangels in individual casserole. Spoon portion of seafood mixture over toast. Top with 3 avocado slices; garnish with 2 additional toast triangles.

*To make tarragon toast triangles: combine 1/2 pound softened butter or margarine with 2 teaspoons crushed tarragon. Spread 22 slices of bread. Toast in oven at 400°F. until golden. Cut each slice diagonally into 4 triangles.

SEAFOOD COMBINATION ⟶

Yield: 1 portion (prepared to order)

Ingredients

SHRIMP, breaded, fried	4
FLOUNDER, FILLET, butter-broiled	1
BACKFIN CRABMEAT	2 ounces
TARTAR SAUCE	1 ounce
LETTUCE LEAVES	as needed
LEMON WEDGE	1
COCKTAIL SAUCE	1 ounce

SEAFOOD AU GRATIN

Yield: 18 6-ounce portions

Ingredients

ONION, chopped	1 cup
BUTTER or MARGARINE	2 to 3 tablespoons
CREAM OF CELERY SOUP, CONDENSED	1 50-ounce can
MILK	1-1/4 cups
CHEESE, CHEDDAR, shredded	1 pound
LIQUID HOT PEPPER SEASONING	1/8 teaspoon
SEAFOOD (LOBSTER, CRABMEAT, and SHRIMP), cooked, flaked	3 pounds
PARSLEY, chopped	1/4 cup
BREAD CUBES, soft	1 quart (3 ounces)
BUTTER or MARGARINE, melted	2 ounces

Procedure

1. Saute onion in butter until tender. Blend in soup and milk; stir until smooth.
2. Add cheese and pepper seasoning; heat slowly, stirring until cheese melts.
3. Fold in seafood and parsley. Ladle into individual baking dishes, allowing 6 ounces each.
4. Toss bread cubes in melted butter. Sprinkle on seafood mixture.
5. Bake in oven at 425°F. for 10 minutes or until sauce is bubbling and buttered bread cubes are brown.

Procedure

1. Arrange shrimp and flounder on opposite sides of plate.
2. Place crabmeat and tartar sauce on lettuce at either side.
3. Serve cocktail sauce in small container in center of plate.

SEAFOOD CREOLE

Yield: 32 portions

Ingredients

ONION, thinly sliced	1-1/2 pounds
CELERY, thinly sliced	1-1/4 pounds
GREEN PEPPER, chopped	12 ounces
GARLIC, minced	2 cloves
MARGARINE	5 ounces
FLOUR	3 ounces (3/4 cup)
TOMATOES, CANNED	1 gallon
BAY LEAVES	2
OKRA, cooked, drained	2-1/4 pounds
SALT	3/4 ounce
SUGAR	1 ounce
WORCESTERSHIRE SAUCE	2 tablespoons
FISH, cooked, flaked	1-1/4 pounds
SHRIMP, cooked	1 pound
RICE, cooked, hot	1-1/4 gallons

Procedure

1. Saute vegetables in margarine; cover and steam until almost done.
2. Add flour and mix well. Add tomatoes and bay leaves; cook and stir until slightly thickened. Add okra and seasonings; heat.
3. Add fish and shrimp; heat thoroughly. Remove bay leaves. Serve over rice.

CIOPPINO

Yield: 25 portions

Ingredients	
BUTTER	1/4 pound
ONIONS, finely chopped	3 medium
GREEN PEPPERS, finely chopped	3 medium
CELERY, finely chopped	2 cups
INSTANT GRANULATED GARLIC	3/4 teaspoon
THYME	1/4 teaspoon
ROSEMARY	1/4 teaspoon
TOMATOES	1 No. 10 can
WATER	1 quart
WHITE WINE	1 cup
SALT	as needed
PEPPER	as needed
CRABMEAT	4 pounds
SHRIMP, LARGE, cooked, cleaned	3 pounds
OYSTERS, shucked	25
CLAMS, shucked	50

Procedure

1. Heat butter; add onion, green pepper, and celery. Saute until just tender.
2. Combine with remaining ingredients, except seafood. Simmer, uncovered, 3 hours, stirring occasionally.
3. Add seafood; simmer a few minutes longer, until edges of oysters curl.
4. Serve in individual casseroles or bowls. Accompany with garlic bread.

LOBSTER/SHRIMP MELANGE

Yield: 25 portions

Ingredients

GREEN PEPPER, chopped	1-1/4 cups
or INSTANT CHOPPED GREEN PEPPER*	1/3 cup
ONION, chopped	1-1/4 cups
or INSTANT CHOPPED ONION*	1/4 cup
CELERY, chopped	2-1/2 cups
OLIVES, GREEN, PIMIENTO-STUFFED, sliced	1-1/4 quarts
SHRIMP, cooked, cut in 1/2-inch pieces	2 pounds
LOBSTER MEAT, cut in 1/2-inch pieces	2 pounds
BLACK PEPPER	1 teaspoon
SALT	2 teaspoons
WORCESTERSHIRE SAUCE	1/4 cup
MAYONNAISE	1 quart
BREAD CRUMBS, soft, buttered	2-1/2 cups

*Rehydrate according to label directions. Drain; fluff.

Procedure

1. Combine green pepper, onion, celery, olives, shrimp, and lobster. Toss lightly.

2. Add pepper, salt, and Worcestershire sauce to mayonnaise; blend. Add to seafood mixture; toss to mix.

3. Portion into individual casseroles; top with crumbs. Bake in oven at 350°F. for 30 minutes.

4. Garnish with whole shrimp and sliced stuffed olive, if desired.

PUNJAB PAELLA →

Yield: 30 1-1/2-cup portions

Ingredients	
BRUSSELS SPROUTS, FROZEN	2-1/2 pounds
RICE	2 pounds
CLAMS or MUSSELS (IN SHELLS)	4 pounds
SHRIMP, shelled, deveined	2 pounds
SCALLOPS	2 pounds
CHICKEN BROTH	2 quarts
BUTTER or MARGARINE	8 ounces
CURRY POWDER	1/4 cup
SALT	as needed

SEAFOOD AND MACARONI CASSEROLE

Yield: 24 portions

Ingredients	
MACARONI SHELLS	2 pounds
CREAM of CELERY SOUP, CONDENSED	1 quart
WATER	2 cups
LEMON JUICE	1/4 cup
CHEESE, CHEDDAR, grated	1/2 pound
SOY SAUCE	1-1/2 tablespoons
CRABMEAT, flaked	2 pounds
SHRIMP, cooked, shelled	2 pounds
PARSLEY, chopped	as needed

Procedure

1. Cook macaroni shells in boiling salted water. Drain.
2. Combine soup and water; heat. Add lemon juice, cheese, and soy sauce.
3. Add crabmeat, shrimp, and macaroni.
4. Turn into individual casseroles or a 12-inch by 18-inch by 2-1/2-inch pan. Bake in oven at 375°F. until heated through and bubbly.
5. Garnish with chopped parsley.

Procedure

1. Thaw brussels sprouts just enough to separate.
2. Spread 1 pound rice in each of two 12-inch by 20-inch by 2-1/2-inch pans. Top each with half the sprouts, clams, shrimp, and scallops.
4. Heat broth to boiling. Add butter, curry, and salt; stir until butter melts. Pour over mixture in pans, dividing evenly.
5. Cover pans with aluminum foil, sealing tightly. Bake in oven at 375°F. for 50 to 60 minutes. Uncover; fluff rice with forks.
6. Serve in individual casseroles.

DEVILED SHRIMP AND TUNA

Yield: 48 portions

Ingredients

BUTTER or MARGARINE, melted	1 pound
BREAD CRUMBS, dry	1-3/4 pounds
APPLESAUCE	1 No. 10 can
BUTTER or MARGARINE, soft	1 pound
PARSLEY, chopped	3/4 cup
LEMON JUICE	1 cup
HORSERADISH	1-1/2 cups
MAYONNAISE	1-1/2 cups
SALT	3 tablespoons
SHRIMP, cooked, cleaned	2 pounds
TUNA, CANNED, broken in large pieces	4 pounds
EGGS, hard-cooked, chopped	24

Procedure

1. Add melted butter to bread crumbs; toss to mix. Set aside.
2. Combine remaining ingredients; mix well.
3. Fill individual casseroles or shells, using No. 16 scoop. Top with buttered crumbs.
4. Bake in oven at 400°F. for 20 minutes. Serve with tartar sauce, if desired.

SEAFOOD NEWBURG

Yield: 6-1/2 quarts, approximately 35 6-ounce portions

Ingredients	
BUTTER or MARGARINE	1 pound
FLOUR	1/2 pound
WATER or STOCK	2 quarts
MILK	2 quarts
SALT	2 tablespoons
WHITE PEPPER	1/4 teaspoon
CAYENNE PEPPER	1/4 teaspoon
PAPRIKA	1 tablespoon
LIQUID HOT PEPPER SEASONING (optional)	1 teaspoon
EGG YOLKS	1/2 cup (6 to 8)
CREAM, HEAVY	2 cups
LOBSTER MEAT, cooked	4-1/2 pounds
SHRIMP, cooked	1-1/2 pounds
SHERRY, DRY	1/4 cup

Procedure

1. Melt butter; blend in flour.
2. Combine water and milk; heat. Add flour mixture; stir vigorously until smooth. Cook and stir about 5 minutes.
3. Add seasonings; mix well. Add a few tablespoons of hot sauce to egg yolks; mix until smooth. Add beaten yolks to sauce; mix well.
4. Reduce heat to low or very low. Stir in cream. Add cooked, cut-up seafood; heat until mixture is heated through. (Avoid over-stirring in order to keep fish pieces whole.) Blend in sherry; place in bain-marie to keep hot.

Note

Other combinations of seafood include: (1) lobster, crab, and shrimp; (2) solid flesh whitefish and shrimp; and (3) canned tuna and crabmeat.

SEAFOOD MELANGE

Yield: 48 portions

Ingredients	
SCALLOPS	8 pounds
WATER, boiling, salted	3 quarts
ONIONS, LARGE, chopped	8
GARLIC	16 cloves
CARAWAY SEEDS	5 tablespoons
CLOVES, WHOLE	1 tablespoon
PEPPERCORNS, WHOLE	1 teaspoon
SHRIMP, SMALL	8 pounds
RICE, cooked	1-1/2 gallons
ALMONDS, SLIVERED, toasted, minced	1 quart
LIQUID from COOKING SCALLOPS and SHRIMP	2 quarts, 2-2/3 cups
CREAM OF CELERY SOUP, CONDENSED	2-3/4 quarts

Procedure

1. Add scallops to boiling salted water; simmer 8 to 10 minutes. Remove from water with slotted spoon. Drain scallops if necessary, returning liquid to the cooking pot.
2. Add onions, garlic, caraway seeds, cloves, and peppercorns to the water. Add shrimp; simmer, covered, 2 to 5 minutes. Drain shrimp; strain and reserve liquid.
3. Shell and devein shrimp. Divide shrimp and scallops into two 12-inch by 18-inch baking pans or 48 individual casseroles.
4. Combine rice and almonds. Spoon over scallops and shrimp.
5. Combine reserved liquid and cream of celery soup. Pour over rice, allowing a scant 2-3/4 quarts to each of the two pans or 3-1/2 ounces per casserole.
6. Bake, uncovered, in oven at 350°F. for 25 minutes.

Seafood Extraordinaire

Western Growers Association

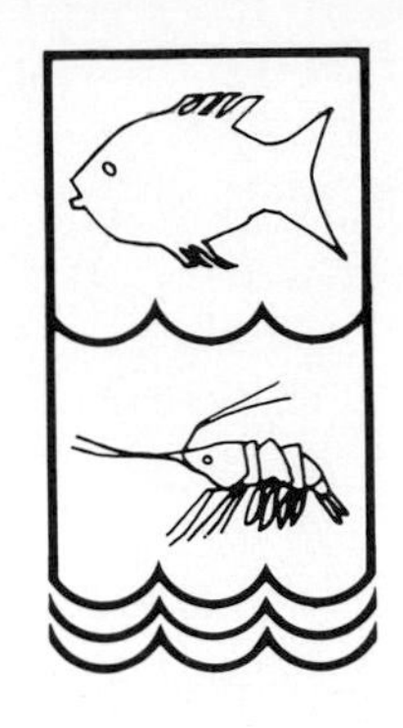

Presentation

THERE IS A VAST storehouse of variety that can be introduced through innovative approaches to presentation. Try new sauces, garnishes, and other go-alongs. Experiment with new plate arrangements. Introduce something pleasingly different in the line of serving equipment.

When feasible, take advantage of the many attractive utensils that make it possible to cook fish individually and bring the sizzling serving to the table in the same pan in which it was cooked. The procedure permits impression-making fanfare. At the same time, it keeps the fish hot, looking its prettiest, tasting its best.

Garnish for Fish *(Onion Slice topped by Pimiento Slice with Watercress color sparks Plate)*

Bureau of Commercial Fisheries, USDA

Fish for Garnish *(Anchovy Crown Salad)*

Credit: American Dairy Association

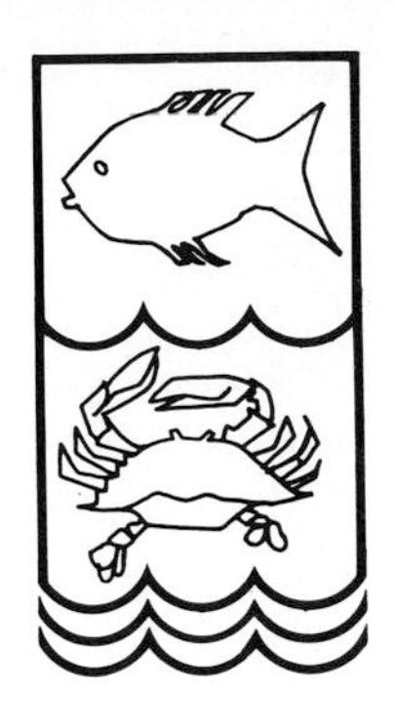

Garnishes

THERE IS NOTHING QUITE like the eye-catching appeal of an effective garnish. Do not ever forget the marvelous alliance between fish and lemon. But add a pleasant surprise—use another garnish as well!

TO SPRINKLE ON FISH:

Sauteed slivered almonds
Chopped parsley
Grated cheese
Sauteed coconut shreds
A few capers
Bits of crisp bacon
Chopped chives
A dash of paprika
Strips or small dice of pimiento
Sauteed chopped ripe olives
Crumbled bleu cheese
Sauteed herb-flavored crumbs
Snipped fresh dill
Sieved hard-cooked egg yolk

TO DRESS UP THE PLATE:

A wedge of lemon
  Edged with paprika
  Dipped in chopped parsley
A wedge of lime
A spray of watercress
Slices of cucumber

A sprig of parsley
Carrot curls
A radish with a few small leaves left intact
Dill, sour or sweet pickle fans
A few cherry tomatoes (whole or halves)
Slices of pickled beet
Parsley-topped grilled tomato half
Sauteed mushroom caps
A spiced peach half
Marinated tomato wedges with chopped parsley or chives
Preserved kumquats on chicory
Mustard pickles in small lettuce cup
Whole cranberry sauce or jelly
A souffle cup of corn relish
A small bunch of green grapes
Marinated orange slices on a bed of cress
A slice of pineapple topped with green pepper slaw
A small mold of tomato aspic, cucumber and lime, or beet and horseradish salad
Broiled orange and grapefruit sections

Fruit Garnish for Breaded Fish Portion

Blue Waters Seafoods Company

Sauces

FISH COOKED by any method takes on new dimensions when dressed or presented with a well-chosen, well-prepared sauce.

Several types of sauces complement the delicate flavor of fish, add a touch of color, or a bit of crunch. A simple butter sauce or maitre d'hotel butter is a perfect complement to sauteed fillets of sole or other delicate, white-fleshed fish. Butter-sauteed almonds make an elegant sauce for sauteed trout and for baked or broiled salmon or halibut. Hollandaise sauce adds a nice fillip to poached fish. It is especially pleasing with rolled fillets. A veloute sauce, made with the seasoned stock in which the fish was poached, is another type of sauce that sets poached fish apart with its own distinguishing touch.

Sauces that have a mayonnaise base make a splendid accompaniment for sauteed or fried fish. They also work out well for poached fish when presented chilled. Tartar sauce goes well with hot, crisp-crusted fried fish of any kind.

Tomato sauces offer an excellent variation for baked halibut, haddock, or cod. There are dozens of other sauces that you can add to the list, including cream sauce with additions of parsley, pimiento, or finely chopped egg; sweet-sour sauces; and some of the sauces made with fruit.

Think of consistency as well as flavor when selecting sauces. For example, fish prepared with a breading calls for a sauce with sufficient body to cling to the fish yet not soak the crust. Melted butters and other thin sauces that team so well with fish cooked without breading do not go at all with offerings of fried fish that feature a crisp golden crust.

Fish Sauced Three Ways

Cod with Shrimp Sauce Veronique; left, Poached Cod with Herb Sauce Macadamia; bottom, Poached Cod with Sauce Marinara.

National Fisheries Institute

Chilled Fillet, Mayonnaise Sauce Verte

Bureau of Commerical Fisheries , USDA

LIME COCKTAIL SAUCE

Yield: 4-3/4 cups

Ingredients

CHILI SAUCE or CATSUP	1 quart
LIME JUICE	1/2 cup
HORSERADISH	1/4 cup
SALT	2 teaspoons
LIQUID HOT PEPPER SEASONING	1/2 teaspoon

Procedure

1. Mix all ingredients; chill.
2. Serve over shrimp or other seafood.

COCKTAIL SAUCE

Yield: approximately 4-1/2 gallons

Ingredients

CATSUP	26 pounds
HORSERADISH	8 pounds
WORCESTERSHIRE SAUCE	5-1/2 ounces

Procedure

Combine ingredients. Chill.

COCKTAIL SAUCE FOR CRABMEAT

Yield: approximately 1 gallon

Ingredients

HORSERADISH	12 ounces (1-1/2 cups)
WORCESTERSHIRE SAUCE	1/4 cup
LEMON JUICE	2 tablespoons
LIQUID HOT PEPPER SEASONING	1 teaspoon
CATSUP, EXTRA HEAVY	1 No. 10 can

Procedure

Combine all ingredients. Chill.

SAUCE LAMAZE

Yield: 1 quart

Ingredients

MAYONNAISE, THICK	2 cups
CHILI SAUCE	2/3 cup
INDIA RELISH, drained	1/2 cup
EGGS, hard-cooked, riced or finely chopped	2
WORCESTERSHIRE SAUCE	1-1/2 teaspoons
CELERY, minced	1/4 cup
CHIVES, minced	2 teaspoons
GREEN PEPPER, minced	2 teaspoons
PIMIENTO, finely chopped	2 teaspoons
BLACK PEPPER	dash
MONOSODIUM GLUTAMATE	1 teaspoon

Procedure

Have mayonnaise at room temperature; fold in all ingredients lightly. Correct seasoning, if necessary.

SAUCE MARINARA

Yield: 1 quart

Ingredients

OLIVE OIL or SALAD OIL	1/4 cup
TOMATOES, CANNED, drained, chopped	1 quart
GARLIC, mashed	1 large clove
PARSLEY, finely chopped	2 teaspoons
OREGANO	1 teaspoon
SALT	1 teaspoon
PEPPER	dash

Procedure

1. Heat oil; add remaining ingredients. Simmer 20 to 30 minutes.
2. Serve over hot poached or steamed fish.

BASIC CHEDDAR CHEESE SAUCE

Yield: 1-1/8 gallons

Ingredients

BUTTER	1 pound, 2 ounces
FLOUR	12 ounces
SALT	1 tablespoon
PAPRIKA	1 tablespoon
WHITE PEPPER	3/4 teaspoon
MILK, scalded	3 quarts
CHEESE, AGED CHEDDAR, shredded	2-1/4 pounds

Procedure

1. Melt butter in heavy saucepan or steam-jacketed kettle; blend in flour and seasonings. Simmer, stirring constantly with a wire whip, about 5 minutes.
2. Add hot milk gradually; stir and cook until thickened and no starch flavor remains, about 15 minutes.
3. Remove from heat; stir in cheese, stirring until cheese melts and sauce is smooth.

Note

To store, cover closely; refrigerate.

CHEDDAR CHEESE SAUCE FOR FISH

Yield: approximately 1 gallon

Ingredients

BASIC CHEDDAR CHEESE SAUCE	3 quarts
MILK	3 cups
SWEET PICKLE RELISH, drained	3 cups
CELERY SEED	1 tablespoon
LIQUID HOT PEPPER SEASONING	2 to 3 teaspoons

Procedure

1. Blend cheese sauce and milk over moderate heat; stir in pickle relish, celery seed, and hot pepper seasoning.
2. Ladle over portions of baked or broiled cod, haddock, halibut, perch, or whitefish, or over poached flounder or sole.

CREAMY ONION SAUCE

Yield: 2 quarts

Ingredients

ONION, thinly sliced	2-1/2 cups (12 ounces)
BUTTER or MARGARINE	3 ounces
CREAM of CELERY SOUP, CONDENSED	1 50-ounce can
MILK	1-2/3 cups
BAY LEAF, WHOLE	1 large

Procedure

1. Saute onion in butter until lightly browned.
2. Blend in soup and milk. Add bay leaf. Bring to a boil; simmer 5 minutes to blend flavors.
3. Remove bay leaf. Serve on broiled, poached,or baked trout.

SWEET AND SOUR SAUCE

Yield: 1-1/2 quarts

Ingredients

APPLE JUICE	3 cups
VINEGAR	1 cup
SUGAR	1 cup
CATSUP	1/2 cup
COOKING OIL	1/4 cup
SOY SAUCE	1 tablespoon
SALT	1/2 teaspoon
CARROTS, sliced diagonally	2 cups
GREEN PEPPER, diced	1 cup
GREEN ONIONS, sliced diagonally	1/2 cup
CORNSTARCH	1/2 cup
APPLE JUICE	1/2 cup

Procedure

1. Combine first amount of apple juice, vinegar, sugar, catsup, oil, soy sauce, and salt. Heat to boiling.
2. Add carrots; cook 15 minutes. Add green pepper and onion; cook 5 minutes longer.
3. Blend cornstarch and remaining apple juice. Add to hot mixture; cook and stir until thickened. Serve with breaded fish portions or fish sticks, or hot broiled shrimp kabobs.

RIPE OLIVE TARTAR SAUCE

Yield: 3 cups

Ingredients

OLIVES, RIPE	1 cup
MAYONNAISE	2 cups
SWEET or DILL PICKLES, chopped or SWEET PICKLE RELISH	1/4 cup
PARSLEY, chopped	1/2 cup
ONION, finely chopped	2 tablespoons

Procedure

1. Cut olives into small wedges.
2. Combine ingredients; chill several hours to thoroughly blend flavors.

HOT TARTAR SAUCE

Yield: 2-1/4 quarts

Ingredients

CREAM OF CELERY SOUP, CONDENSED	1 51-ounce can
MAYONNAISE	2 cups
WATER	1 to 1-1/2 cups
OLIVES, stuffed, chopped	1/4 cup
SWEET PICKLE RELISH	1/4 cup
PARSLEY, chopped	2 tablespoons
ONION, minced	2 tablespoons

Procedure

1. Combine soup and mayonnaise; stir until smooth.
2. Blend in water, a small amount at a time. Add remaining ingredients; heat.
3. Serve with fried or broiled fish or scallops.

REMOULADE SAUCE I

Yield: 1-1/4 gallons

Ingredients

MAYONNAISE (TART)	1 gallon
GARLIC, finely minced	16 cloves
TARRAGON, DRIED	1/3 cup
EGGS, hard-cooked, finely chopped	16
DIJON or DUSSELDORF MUSTARD	1/3 cup
ANCHOVY PASTE	1/3 cup
PARSLEY, chopped	1 cup

Procedure

1. Combine ingredients, blending well.
2. Let stand (refrigerated) before serving to allow flavors to blend.

REMOULADE SAUCE II

Yield: 1 quart

Ingredients

MAYONNAISE	2-1/2 cups
OLIVES, RIPE, drained, chopped	1-1/2 cups
DILL PICKLE, chopped	1/2 cup
CAPERS, drained, chopped	1/4 cup
PARSLEY, chopped	1/4 cup
CHIVES, chopped	1/4 cup
PREPARED MUSTARD	1-1/2 tablespoons
TARRAGON WINE VINEGAR	1 tablespoon
TARRAGON, DRIED, CRUMBLED	2 teaspoons

Procedure

1. Combine ingredients; mix well.
2. Allow to stand 1 hour or longer to blend flavors.

FISH SAUCE

Yield: approximately 1 quart

Ingredients

MAYONNAISE	2-1/2 cups
SOUR CREAM	1-1/4 cups
LEMON JUICE, fresh	3 tablespoons
CHILI SAUCE	1/3 cup
PAPRIKA	2-1/2 teaspoons
WHITE PEPPER	1-1/4 teaspoons
SALT	2 teaspoons
CAYENNE PEPPER	1/4 teaspoon

Procedure

1. Combine all ingredients; beat until blended.
2. Chill. Serve over hot or chilled cooked fish or over seafood salads.

GOURMET FISH SAUCE

Yield: approximately 1-1/4 gallons

Ingredients

CUCUMBERS	5 pounds
SOUR CREAM	2-1/2 quarts
ONION, finely chopped	1-1/2 cups
LEMON JUICE	1/4 cup
HORSERADISH	1/3 cup
SALT	1 tablespoon
PEPPER	1/2 teaspoon
PAPRIKA	1 teaspoon

Procedure

1. Peel cucumbers; remove seeds. Grate coarsely. (There should be 2 quarts grated cucumber.)
2. Combine with remaining ingredients; mix gently until well blended.
3. Chill several hours.

CUCUMBER SAUCE

Yield: approximately 1 quart

Ingredients

MAYONNAISE*	1-1/2 cups
SALT	1-1/2 teaspoons
CELERY SEED	1-1/2 teaspoons
CUCUMBER, finely diced	3 cups

*Equal parts mayonnaise and commercial sour cream may be substituted.

Procedure

Combine mayonnaise, salt, and celery seed. Add cucumber; chill. Serve with fried fish or scallops or with cold lobster or shrimp.

KRAUT-APPLE SAUCE FOR FISH

Yield: approximately 3-3/4 quarts

Ingredients

KRAUT, undrained	2 pounds
APPLESAUCE	4 pounds
HORSERADISH	2 cups
APPLES, RED, UNPARED, chopped	8 ounces

Procedure

1. Cut kraut into short lengths.
2. Combine with remaining ingredients; mix well. Chill.

LEMON BUTTER

Yield: 50 portions

Ingredients

LEMON JUICE	1 cup
BUTTER, melted	1-1/2 pounds
PAPRIKA	2 teaspoons
PARSLEY, chopped	1 cup

Procedure

Mix ingredients together.

HERBED LEMON BUTTER

Yield: 1 pound

Ingredients

BUTTER	1 pound
LEMON RIND, grated	2 tablespoons
OREGANO, CRUSHED	1/2 teaspoon
ROSEMARY, CRUSHED	1/2 teaspoon
THYME, CRUSHED	1/2 teaspoon
LEMON JUICE, fresh	1/3 cup

Procedure

1. Cream butter on mixer, using paddle attachment. Add grated lemon rind and herbs.
2. Gradually add lemon juice, continuing to mix until all liquid is absorbed.
3. Form mixture into sticks or blocks; chill until firm. Slice into pats for serving on broiled fish.

SEASONED LEMON BUTTER

Yield: 1 pound

Ingredients

BUTTER	1 pound
LEMON RIND	1 to 2 tablespoons
WORCESTERSHIRE SAUCE	1 tablespoon
LEMON JUICE, fresh	1/3 cup

Procedure

1. Cream butter on mixer, using paddle attachment. Add grated lemon rind.
2. Gradually add Worcestershire and lemon juice, continuing to mix until all liquid is absorbed.
3. Form mixture into sticks or blocks; chill until firm.
4. Slice into pats to serve on broiled fish or lobster.

LIME HOLLANDAISE SAUCE

Yield: 2 cups

Ingredients

EGG YOLKS	8
SALT	1 teaspoon
DRY MUSTARD	1 teaspoon
SUGAR	1 teaspoon
LIQUID HOT PEPPER SEASONING	1/2 teaspoon
BUTTER, melted	2 cups (1 pound)
LIME JUICE	1/2 cup

Procedure

1. Beat egg yolks until thick and lemon-colored; add salt, mustard, sugar, and liquid hot pepper seasoning.
2. Add 1 cup of the melted butter a small amount at a time, beating constantly.
3. Combine remaining melted butter with lime juice. Add to egg yolk mixture a small amount at a time, beating constantly.
4. Serve with broiled fish, poached salmon, or flounder.

HERB SAUCE MACADAMIA

(See picture, page 218)

Yield: approximately 1-1/2 quarts

Ingredients

BUTTER or MARGARINE	1-1/2 pounds
SCALLIONS, finely chopped	8
FINES HERBES (THYME, OREGANO, SAGE, ROSEMARY, MARJORAM and BASIL)	1/3 cup
MACADAMIA NUTS, chopped*	3 cups
WHITE WINE	3 cups

*For a filbert version, substitute chopped filberts.

Procedure

1. Melt butter. Add scallions, seasonings, and nuts; saute lightly.
2. Add wine; heat.
3. Serve over hot poached or steamed fish.

TOMATO SAUCE FOR FISH

Yield: 3-1/2 quarts

Ingredients

BUTTER or MARGARINE	12 ounces
CELERY, finely chopped	1-1/2 cups
ONION, finely chopped	1-1/2 cups
GREEN PEPPER, finely chopped	1-1/2 cups
TOMATO SAUCE	1 No. 10 can

Procedure

1. Melt butter; add celery, onion, and green pepper. Saute until soft but not brown.
2. Add tomato sauce; heat.

OLIVE TOMATO SAUCE

Yield: 1 quart

Ingredients

OLIVES, RIPE, chopped	2 cups
TOMATOES CANNED	1 quart
INSTANT MINCED ONION	2 tablespoons
PARSLEY, chopped	1/4 cup
VINEGAR	2 tablespoons
SUGAR	2 tablespoons
SWEET BASIL	1 teaspoon
THYME	1/2 teaspoon
GARLIC SALT	1 teaspoon
CORNSTARCH	2 tablespoons
WATER	2 tablespoons

Procedure

1. Combine olives, tomatoes, and seasonings. Bring to a boil; reduce heat; simmer 15 minutes.
2. Blend cornstarch and water. Stir into sauce; cook and stir until sauce thickens. Serve hot or cold with fish sticks or breaded fish portions.

SOUR CREAM DILL SAUCE

Yield: 1 quart

Ingredients

SOUR CREAM	3 cups
OLIVES, RIPE, CANNED, SLICED, drained	1-1/2 cups
CHIVES, chopped	1/4 cup
SALT	1 teaspoon
DILL WEED	1 teaspoon
PARSLEY, chopped	2 tablespoons

Procedure

1. Combine ingredients; mix well.
2. Allow to stand 1 hour or longer to blend flavors.

SHRIMP SAUCE VERONIQUE

(See picture, page 218)

Yield: approximately 1-1/2 quarts

Ingredients

GRAPES, WHITE, SMALL, SEEDLESS	2 cups
WATER	1 cup
WHITE SAUCE, prepared with fish stock	1 quart
SHRIMP, TINY, cooked	12 ounces
CREAM, HEAVY	1/2 cup
SALT	as needed
PEPPER	as needed

Procedure

1. Simmer grapes in water for 2 to 3 minutes; drain.
2. Heat white sauce; fold in shrimp.
3. Whip cream; fold into sauce mixture. Add drained grapes. Season with salt and pepper.
4. Serve hot, over poached or steamed fish.

INDEX